WHO THE F*CK SAYS WE HAVE TOMORROW?

How I made cancer my bitch!

A Memoir

MARYSE LAFLAMME

Copyright© 2022 by Maryse Laflamme. All formats of the book first published in 2022 by MARYSE LAFLAMME.

All rights reserved. No part of this book may be reproduced, distributed, or transmitted in any form or by any means, including photocopying, recording, or other electronic or mechanical methods, without the prior written permission of the author, except in the case of brief quotations embodied in critical reviews and certain other noncommercial uses permitted by copyright law. For permission requests, please contact the author at https://maryselaflamme.com.

First Edition, January 2023

ISBNs:

Ebook: 978-1-7351721-3-2

Paperback: 978-1-7351721-2-5

Hardback: 978-1-7351721-8-7

Printed in the United States of America

This is a work of nonfiction. Names, characters, places, and incidents either are products of the author's memory or are used fictitiously. Any resemblance to actual persons, living or dead, events, or locales is entirely coincidental.

ATTENTION: SCHOOLS AND BUSINESSES

Publisher is happy to offer special discounts on bulk purchases of this book for educational, business, or sales promotional use. For information, please complete the contact form at https://MaryseLaflamme.com.

Contents

IMPORTANT NOTE	VII
Dedication	IX
Prologue	5
PART I	9
1. After the Event	11
2. In Real Life	17
3. The Event	29
4. Doomed	39
PART II	43
5. There is Fuckery Afoot	45
6. From Tofu to Cherry Garcia	55
7. Guru Hopping	65
8. So Many Tears, So Little Time	77

9.	In Limbo	85
10.	Across the Divide	93
11.	No Getting High	99
12.	Can You See It?	107
13.	Chemo Brain	115
14.	Sometimes the Universe Just Likes to Fuck With You	119
15.	When Death Takes a Pass	125
16.	Lies Lies Lies	135
17.	I Decide	141
PART III		153
18.	Yesterday's Woo-woo is Today's Mainstream	155
19.	Groping Through the Darkness	163
20.	Apathy	169
21.	Stressing it Out	177
22.	I'm a Kintsugi Person	181
23.	Reframing a Picture	187
24.	Just Breathe	191
25.	On Friendship	197
26.	More Shedding	203
27.	Trippin' Out of My Mind	209
28.	Health Freak	217

29. Cleaning out My Emotions	223
30. This is for Me Too	237
31. From Invisible to Visible	243
32. Done With being a Good Girl	249
33. Time on My Mind	253
34. Death	255
35. Repeat Mode	261
36. Into Nothing	265
37. Woo-woo in Real Time	273
38. Miracle Shmiracle	283
Did You Enjoy My Story? You Can Make a Big Difference.	289
Join My Mailing List and Get Free Goodies	291
Acknowledgments	293
About the Author	297
Also by Maryse Laflamme	299

IMPORTANT NOTE

My lawyer wants you to know that I'm not a medical doctor, a psychiatrist, a homeopath, a naturopath, or any other kind of doctor at all. Just a woman who found her way through the quagmire of the myriad healing protocols available to us all and managed to make it work for her. Though there are reference notes, they are there to show you where I got my information. You don't even have to look at them; it's not necessary to the story. I just want you to know that what I say is real. And the lawyer also wants you to know that I am not advising, or encouraging, you to do any of the healing modalities mentioned in the book.

We go woo-woo sometimes in here, yes, but we tread carefully, mindfully, and we only move forward with any healing protocol after discussing it with our medical professionals, and after deciding for ourselves, not because we read about it in a memoir, yes?

Dedicated to:

All those who wish to, and those who have, overcome to create the best versions of themselves.

*

Et comme toujours, à Paul-Henri et Alexanne.

GET THREE FREE "OUTTAKES"
FROM MY FIRST MEMOIR *CROOKED STRAIGHT*
**EXCLUSIVE TO YOU WHEN YOU
JOIN MY (e)MAILING LIST**

Building a relationship with my readers is one of the pleasures of writing. I welcome direct communication with you. Contact me with any question about any of my books, and I'll reply.

What I call the outtakes, something usually reserved for movies, are three short backstories related to my first memoir about the night I helped Toronto police find and arrest a violent serial rapist while there was a warrant out for my own arrest—and while sitting right there for five hours at Toronto Police Headquarters. Without getting caught. In the book, I just touch upon the material in the outtakes, which describe those incidents in detail.

If you sign up to my mailing list, I'll send them to you right away. Plus, occasionally, other goodies.

Click Here to get the outtakes, **for free**, by signing up. (https://dl.bookfunnel.com/wxh8gjs9tn)

Yin and yang, male and female, strong and weak, rigid and tender, heaven and earth, light and darkness, thunder and lightning, cold and warmth, good and evil... the interplay of opposite principles constitutes the universe.

—Confucius

***

For what it's worth: it's never too late or, in my case, too early to be whoever you want to be. There's no time limit; start whenever you want. You can change or stay the same—there are no rules to this thing. We can make the best or the worst of it. I hope you make the best of it. I hope you see things that startle you. I hope you feel things you never felt before. I hope you meet people with a different point of view. I hope you live a life you're proud of. And if you find that you're not, I hope you have the strength to start all over again.

—From The Curious Case of Benjamin Button

Prologue

I nearly titled this book *Phoenix*. But that felt clichéd, even though it's true. My life crashed and burned, and out of the debris, a new me emerged. The ashes of my past shed away with each flap of my new wings.

Instead, I named it *Who the F*ck Says We Have Tomorrow?* because that also is true. Life gives none of us a guarantee of a tomorrow, now does it?

And if I'm going to die sooner rather than later, or even later rather than sooner after all, I choose to go out in style, baby. No more acting like an understudy hoping for her moment to shine, while feeling terrified of it. I got rid of the "terrified" part, walking myself right out into that light.

I made this decision two years after what I call The Event, when life slayed me in five seconds flat, starting with eight broken vertebrae.

And that was the good news.

Once I opted to stick around and thrive, despite that aforementioned lack of guarantee of a tomorrow, digging down to the elemental level to fix things that negatively affected my whole being—and therefore my chances of healing—became a *necessity*. Just like one guts a house before rebuilding, my emotional body and my mind needed excavating. After all, you can't create a life, or anything else, on top of a pile of trash. First, the garbage must go.

For me, that meant peeling away the protective layers around my feelings, like stripping off old drywall. It involved examining each emotion closely, like under a microscope, to determine its validity and origin. Why did I sometimes feel anger instead of just discomfort whenever someone crossed my personal boundaries? Why were my personal boundaries set so far from my physical body? The list of issues I needed to address was long, and tackling it turned out to be the hardest yet most rewarding task I've ever undertaken.

Healing, truly healing, meant changing my thoughts, which transformed my feelings and, eventually, my entire being—mind, body, and soul. I discovered that not only did my physical body need healing, but also my emotional body and mind. There was a lot to unpack, deep scars hiding in the shadows of the remnants of early trauma, painful memories to be obliterated; the necessity to act as my own fairy godmother and zap them away.

That meant dropping ninety percent of my friendships, moving two states away with all my possessions only to give sixty percent of them away once at my destination. It meant revisiting the fundamentals of my family relationships. Scrutinizing and analyzing how I approached, well, everything in life. Like gutting that house, I stripped my life down to its studs.

Right now, I sit at my writing desk, looking out the window of the new house I built while rebuilding myself. The sight of old-growth trees around my property brings me peace. My heart does a small flip of gratitude for everything that led me to this moment. Including the cancer that did its best to kill me. Why, you ask?

Because cancer was the catalyst that compelled me to do what it took to rise from the ashes and create a life of my own deliberate and mindful making. One built on the solid foundation of a well-balanced heart and mind. No more garbage!

In the process of healing my soul, my mind healed, and my body naturally followed.

But I couldn't have done it without having learned to love myself—learned to love life itself.

Pain and struggle might shatter our complacency and compel us to evolve, but it's love that breathes life into the transformation and makes every hard-won moment worth living.

PART I

THE EVENT

After the Event

In the early spring of 2018, I sit, teetering on the edge of a rehabilitation hospital bed. An IV tube hangs from my left arm; the machine to which it should be attached beeps away, distracting me, doing its best to drag my mind out of the fog into which it disappeared weeks ago. It only peers out when outside forces demand it. This is one of those times.

What's pulling me out of the fog stands in front of me in spearmint-colored hospital scrubs, tall as an oak tree, and with the same girth. He offers me both his arms, holding them out like rails. The sheer strength of him fascinates me.

How is he able to hold his arms up so effortlessly? Why can everyone around, but me, move easily? Walking, bending, twisting, reaching, sitting? A faint memory of having once been able to do the same comes to me. I had that ability, too.

But it's gone now. Tears cloud my vision.

He looks so powerful; it's intimidating. I look away from the intensity of his strength like from a bright noon sun.

The fog lifts some, the buzzing in my ear recedes. My body adapts itself to sitting instead of reclining against the elevated back of this bed, my usual posture for the past seven weeks. Or is that eight? Or ten?

Until two days ago when we tried this exercise for the first time, my legs hadn't hung off the side of a bed, or anything else, since my admission to the first hospital out of the three I've been in so far.

I hear dinging. What is it? I know that sound; just can't place it. It irritates me, both because of the noise it makes and because what it might be scratches at me like a dog scratching the door to be let out. The noise threatens to pull me out of my self-imposed retreat into the foggy back of my mind. It goes on. *Ding, beep, ding, beep.* What is it? A metronome? But what would that be doing here? Plus, the sound is too sharp for it to be that. My mind keeps reaching but keeps coming up empty.

Then, I realize it comes from the medical machinery next to my bed from which I've been unhooked for this exercise. I guess it wonders where my IV line is at, the thing into which it's supposed to pump fluids.

"All right, Maryse, ready to do this thing with me?" says the physical therapist, the tall oak. Chris. I think that's his name but can't recall for sure. Opioid brain.

He ignores the dinging. I seem to be the only one who notices, the only one it bothers. Having never been big on asking for help, I remain silent about it.

Chris braces himself to be able to support me should I shock both of us and stand, the purpose of his presence in my room.

Recalling the alternative—never walking again—something compels me to grasp his arms, as hard as I can, even harder now, gripping the rails they've become with all I've got in me as if gripping, instead of pushing down on, will help me get myself to a standing position.

In a rush, the pain shoots from my mid- and lower back in all directions—the feeling that of bones, ligaments, and tendons being torn apart by a wild beast, a tiger, a lion. An electric current courses through all of me. The pain comes not only because of what I'm attempting to do, but because my pain meds have been scaled back to try and alleviate the nausea that occurs each time I attempt to do this.

Out loud, I only moan, while my brain short-circuits, unable to cope with what my physical body is enduring. *Damn, damn, damn, I can't do this, I can't do it.*

TRY! screams some part of me.

A cart rattles by in the hallway outside my door, which has been left open. An announcement comes over a pager down the hall. I think I smell myself, an acrid smell, then a metallic taste in my mouth: fear. I don't want this to be my life.

Please!

Again. All my strength behind the effort—now. *Let's go, let's go, let's GO.* I push down on his arms, exhaling every last ounce of air from my lungs to propel myself upward.

Nothing.

Tears blur my vision. My heart pounds away, a galloping horse who wants out, out of the pain, the misery, the...hopelessness that has engulfed me since my diagnosis.

I want to stand again more than anything.

Want to walk again more than anything.

More than I want that first-class ticket to London on Virgin Air with a facial and massage on board that I add to my Christmas wish list every year. More than the new hybrid Lexus I coveted before what I've come to think of as The Event. More than I want to find true love, even.

If I can't ever stand and walk again, do I even want any other part of life? Do I?

I've let life happen to me, gone with the flow, lived by the seat of my pants, the same way I sometimes flew single-engine airplanes in my past.

A requirement to get a private pilot's license is a 150 nautical miles (172 miles) solo cross-country flight with three full landings. While on the final leg of the landing pattern at one airport, the air traffic controller advised me that wind shear on the runway had just been reported and I should consider aborting my landing. If caught in wind shear, I could crash and either die or be seriously hurt. I had maybe thirty seconds to decide before gunning it and climbing again if I wasn't going to land.

Taking the gamble, I advised the air traffic controller that I was coming in. All went well, except for a strong wind that tried to push me off the runway once on the ground, which presented no real danger.

But it could have gone the other way. I took similar risks on at least two other occasions.

It's becoming clearer and clearer every day that these strategies—not that they are strategies—won't work to get me out of this.

Do I care?

Dizziness overcomes me and my whole being falls forward into the fog. Out of it, Chris's two arms reach out to steady me as if from a rowboat appearing seconds before I give up and let myself go under.

Except...I think I *want* to let go...

Ding, ding, ding goes the dammed medical machinery again, disturbing me in my cocoon of doom; a second sound on top of the other. *Stop!*

Though I've eaten next to nothing for the past seven or eight weeks, going from 150-some pounds to 115 while subsisting mostly on smoothies because I can't get anything else down, I feel nauseated. My ears buzz again.

Somehow, from out of the fog, part of me realizes that I don't really want the alternative—letting go and sinking—so I reach out, grip those arms, my nails piercing the flesh like bird claws. It must hurt him, I think, and wince.

Suddenly, his voice slams me back into reality.

"Maryse, grab my arms!"

Confused, I realize the arm gripping is only happening in my mind. My hands—both, in fact—grip the edge of the mattress instead.

And I wonder, *Is the struggle even worth it if what that doctor told me is true?*

In Real Life

The next day is Groundhog Day. Again.

"Come on, Maryse. You CAN do it! Just take my arms and push down on them. It's okay. I can handle it!" says Chris the physical therapist, with urgency in his voice but wearing a large smile. A second therapist stands at the foot of my bed, ready to lend a hand, presumably to help catch me if I fall.

If these two think their suave manners will compel me to get out of this bed...

They have both come to my bedside every day for the past week to get me to stand up, turn my body a few inches to my left and sit in the wheelchair waiting right next to the bed for me. In my old life, this would have been a cinch, would have taken all of three seconds. It might have even been fun.

The ticking and beeping of machines that keep people alive in hospitals worldwide filter in from the room across the corridor from mine, providing the background soundtrack for this moment. A nurse has already come in to quiet the machines around my own bed, thankfully, but I know they'll beep again after I lie down, after the nurse hooks me back up after this exercise. Exercise in futility, I think.

A grunt. It's mine. Its guttural aspect surprises me, coming from a place so deep inside, sounding so foreign, that it feels like it's coming from someone other than me.

My breathing sounds like pranayama's breath of fire, a form of yoga: fast, in and out. I grab Chris's arms again, though discouraged and not expecting to make progress.

And, sure enough, still nothing. My butt remains, as if glued there, on the edge of the rehabilitation center bed in which I've lain for two weeks so far, ambulanced here after weeks and weeks in two other hospitals.

By the way, emergency medical technicians, those men and women who drive ambulances and stabilize patients enough to transport them to a hospital, deserve a medal. Especially if they have to deal with me.

During the ambulance ride from my home to the first hospital I was taken to, before my body had been fully saturated with painkillers, pain filled every inch of my body and mind, and had hijacked all my faculties for reasoning.

The ambulance went over a speed bump.

"SLOW. DOWN! *PLEASE!*" I yelled at the driver after I'd breathed through an excruciating spasm brought on by going over the bump.

Why was he going so fast? What was the hurry? I wasn't in danger of dying, as far as I knew.

He'd patiently and gently said, "Ma'am, I'm just doing five miles an hour. Even slower over the bumps."

That shut me up, but also increased my anxiety. If that was so, why did my body go into spasms over a small bump crossed at such a slow speed? It made no sense. The past three days made no sense.

I'd done nothing at all to explain my back hurting this much. Something had gone way awry. Despite having spent three nights sitting up on a dining room chair "sleeping" with my head resting on a bunch of pillows stacked up on the table in front of me, I'd still thought that this would pass; I'd just pulled something, and it would be well soon. That's all. I'd agreed to be taken to the hospital to indulge my children—I didn't really need to go there at all.

The ambulance ride had woken me to the fact that something serious had happened. And that it had been getting worse during the three days since The Event.

Now on this rehab hospital bed, I wonder. Will I ever be able to once again stand like it's nothing? Without thinking of all the effort and gyrations my muscles and bones go through each time? Just stand up and start walking? After nearly a week of trying, I doubt my ability to ever do so again.

Perhaps my physical body is *cooked*, wants out, is done, no more.

The eight compacted fractures in my spine, the reason for my predicament—or rather, the effect of the reason for it—gives my spine and legs a reason for not trying.

With such a thing hanging over my life, what's the point? And the risk of excruciating pain every time I try isn't worth it. Is it?

"Okay, Maryse, we'll try again tomorrow. Good job today! At least you're sitting on the edge of the bed. Progress! I'll see you tomorrow," says Chris, a smile on his face.

He hovers over me while I scoot back—very carefully—into a semi supine position against the elevated head of the bed, my legs back on the bed, sweat pouring down my face. Chris wants to help, but no one can touch me at all unless unavoidable. My rule.

The pain from what appears to be a pinched nerve in my spine, created by one of the collapsed vertebrae, feels like an electric shock zapping every cell in me—even if touched on an arm, or a leg, on any part of me, not just on my back. The spasms equate to large hands tearing apart the muscles of my back and shaking them hard.

Is he serious? Sitting on the edge of the bed is progress? Is he just humoring a hopeless case, me?

Maybe I do want to walk again despite that other piece of news. The smell of the pine trees during my last hike in Zion National Park fills my nostrils, followed by the slightly musty smell of the water mixed with the pungent odor of the ducks at the man-made lake near my home where I used to walk several times per week.

I recall the hiking I've done in my lifetime so far. Most trails in Zion, many trails in Bryce Canyon, the Kalalau Trail on the island of Kauai—considered one of the most beautiful and dangerous trails in the world—while five months pregnant with my son, no less. Trails in Colorado, Nevada, the Saguaro National Park in Arizona, both east and west, crossing the entire Catalina Mountains in one day (foolish plan with friends to do it all downhill to make it possible to do in a day), many trails in Sedona, Massachusetts, New Brunswick, Nova Scotia, Alaska, Colorado, plus countless others I've forgotten.

I cherish the ability to walk as one of the most important reasons for living. For me.

Walks in nature feed my soul, ground me, sustain me. My need to walk in nature feels equivalent to drinking from the faucet in large gulps after a long time without water.

Will I wither and die even sooner without it?

Some deep part of me seems to think so. Therefore, like a baby learning how for the first time, I can't give up.

That night, I remember something. I might not be able to stand up and walk in real life, but I *can* do it in my head. Visualization works for athletes preparing for a match or a game. It can work for me in preparation for walking again.

Encouraged by that, over four days with no physical therapy because of a long weekend, I play it over and over in my head like a film loop stuck on repeat. I see myself sitting up in bed, hanging my legs over the side, grabbing the arms of the physical therapist, and smoothly standing up like a queen accepting the help of a gentleman to stand from her throne.

But, there are the drugs, too. They sap what energy I might have without them. Morphine, oxycodone, and a strong anti spasm medication are administered to me several times during the day and twice during the night. I welcome them with my whole being, me who'd once held world summits in my head before for days before taking any prescription drug.

Five days a week, Chris comes to my room, sometimes on his own, sometimes with an assistant, encouraging me to stand and get into that wheelchair.

"You CAN do it!" he repeats ad nauseam.

What did he think he was doing? Me, get out of this bed and into that chair? With eight broken vertebrae, with those excruciating spasms that strangle my ability to even breathe when they attack?

"I just can't...," I whine.

And immediately hate myself for it. Hate that life put me into a position that compels me to whine.

This has been the gist of our physical therapy sessions each day for more than a week.

After days of trying, I feel confused by my failure.

"I don't understand. I've only been in bed for, I don't know, seven weeks, eight weeks? Just eight weeks! Why have my legs stopped working?" I ask, frustration and confusion lacing every word, oozing from my every pore.

"It's normal. You broke your back. You'll stand up again if you really want to."

If I really want to? Like it's a choice?

Rain hitting the window by my bed distracts me, surprises me. This is Vegas; rain falls rarely. It mimics my state of mind, where tears form the background to all my thoughts these days.

"You're ready. Your bones have healed enough to at least get started. Come on, give it a shot. I can pull you up if you want."

"NO! No pulling!"

Why is he even saying that? He knows better. He follows up with more encouragement.

"You CAN do it." "Just push down on my arms. PUSH HARDER!"

If he says "you can do it" one more time...

No way will I allow him to pull me up. I fear the spasms as much as plane crashes, nights alone in dark forests teeming with cobras and lions and bears, or standing on the edge of a bridge looking down, and feeling the sensation of my back breaking again.

I sleep partially awake, afraid a nurse will come in and try to move me or move the head of my bed up or down without warning. I allow no one to touch me or the controls of my bed out of fear of those spasms.

Even with all my rules to avoid them, spasms come anyway, uninvited, badly behaved, several times each day, despite the strong antispam medication I swallow religiously six times per day, which means waking up every four hours. And no relying on the nurses to keep the schedule! I set my alarm day and night to be sure those meds travel down my throat on the four-hour dot.

Now, I sit on the edge of the bed, my legs over the side, hands grasping the mattress. With my eyes closed as tight as possible, jaw locked, I grab all my remaining strength and courage and slowly push myself up to a standing position. For a mere second or so, mind you, counting to one, one thousand, at most, but I DO IT. I'm sitting in the wheelchair. Ecstasy overwhelms me as I get back into bed, my whole body shaking. Nausea collides with joy inside me, pushing back from one another as the strangers they are.

Lying back in my usual near-supine position, the top sheet somehow tangled around my legs, I smile.

Maybe now I could do it in real life.

Yes, this happened only in my mind.

On Day Four of having lived the scene in my head, the therapists arrive at my bedside, no doubt ready for the same resistance from me.

They have no idea what's coming. Me neither for that matter, but nevertheless, the idea of shocking them by standing makes me chuckle.

We start with the usual routine. Chris tells me, "You CAN do it!" as I teeter there on the edge while he probably expects me to whine that I can't.

I move my hands back a couple of inches from the edge of the mattress, then fist and shove them into the mattress to push myself up without his help, unlike in my visualization. But, I do. I stand!

I DO it! This time, in real life. IRL!

I stand exactly how I'd visualized it.

Because I sway like a flag in a strong wind, I latch onto Chris's extended arms, just as he grabs me by my armpits to keep me from falling. That's when I realize that maybe it's okay for others to touch me sometimes. For the first time, there's no spasm from his touch. But, in a flash, standing and sitting overtake that thought. For a brief moment, Chris forgets to keep a neutral face, and I glimpse his shock at my action. Silent laughter bubbles up in me. I got him!

With a grunt, I turn slightly to my left and drop down into the waiting wheelchair, never pausing while upright for even a second. I do it like a ballet dancer in *Swan Lake* going from a position on the floor to standing *en pointe* in one fluid motion. Okay, no, I'm nowhere near as fluid as a ballerina, more like a puppet at the hands of an inexperienced puppet master, my limbs all akimbo. But still.

I cry, hyperventilate, and feel so dizzy I think I'll fall out of the chair.

"I've got you," says Chris, standing directly in front of me and as close as he can to keep me from toppling forward, his hands ready to hold me by my shoulders. "Breathe," he adds.

"I...can't...," I say. Unable to speak, I nod toward the bed.

We repeat the exercise in reverse, this time from the wheelchair to the bed.

All told, in less than two minutes, back in bed, I burst into tears, and grin so wide my face might break.

I DID IT! OMG! I did it!

"Great JOB, Maryse!" says Chris, now standing at the foot of my bed, grinning so wide that his face might crack open, too.

Chris and his assistant, John, share a look and I understand that they didn't expect me to do this today.

"Hey, congrats," John says to me, smiling. He leaves since he's no longer needed, and Chris, after a few instructions and a promise to come back tomorrow for more fun, leaves, too. I bask in my victory.

My eyes go to the tree outside my window. For some reason, gazing at it gives me peace, gives me strength. I want to share my victory with it. *Did you see that?!*

A nurse comes in and hooks me back up to the IV machine and also congratulates me.

Those two minutes exhausted me. I drift off thinking of how sitting in a chair is a most interesting activity. Something that, like most of us, I've never noticed before, but now find fascinating. Having the ability to stand is a miracle, in my opinion. Never have I appreciated the ability to do so more.

Putting one foot in front of the other and taking ourselves from one spot to another is, drumroll, an *effin'* miracle, pardon *mon français*, and the cliché.

I sleep for four hours and wake up just in time to take the drugs that keep me from screaming in agony.

By then, I've been on my back, heavily sedated, on the beds of three different hospitals over a period of about eight weeks.

When I wake, the triumph is my first thought.

The second is whether it matters. Because that other thing, what that doctor told me?

It sucks all the pleasure out of my win.

The Event

"The Event," as I've come to refer to the incident in question, occurred on the morning following the evening on which I gave myself a strong talking-to about finding and calling a doctor first thing the next morning.

I'd spent the night in a reclining position on my couch because getting out of bed proved too difficult due to extreme back pain. It turned into an exercise in logistics I wouldn't wish on anyone.

When I woke up—or rather, roused myself from quasi sleep—I thought, you know, seems to be better today, doesn't hurt as much. Until my world tilted on its axis, dark clouds gathered, and the whole thing came crashing down.

Strangely, I felt frozen in time and in place, in a half-standing position, hands at my back. I'd later think it would have made more sense if I'd crumpled to the floor.

As eight of my vertebrae broke and collapsed—though I didn't know yet that this was what had happened—I heard a sound so piercing, so wrenching, so guttural that it distracted me momentarily. Then, I realized that this inhumane sound had come from me—was coming from me.

My scream brought a friend, who'd been staying over, rushing into the living room from the guest room on the other side of my condo. He stopped dead in his tracks and blanched when he saw me.

In the end, he called 911. Somehow, with both hands grabbing the banister, and going down one step, taking a break, then walking down the next step, taking a break, and so on, spasms gripping my back at nearly each step, I made it down to an ambulance; they didn't have an evacuation chair, and anyway, the likelihood of me getting into one at that point was iffy. I also wouldn't let the EMTs touch me to put me on the gurney. I already knew that touch was unbearable after my friend had tried to take my arm to help me sit.

An x-ray was taken and the results showed eight broken vertebrae, but strangely the doctor didn't admit me even though there was no logical reason for this to have happened. He said I'd broken my back, but that he couldn't put a cast around vertebrae, so go home and rest, and take this pain medication, he said, while handing me a prescription.

Something didn't ring right. Why had my vertebrae collapsed? If at least I'd done it zip-lining, skydiving, or rock climbing, or fallen to the ground from a few floors up it would have made more sense. No, it had happened when I'd done something the majority of us do on the regular: I'd gone from sitting to standing.

Another friend came to get me, and there followed another excruciating motor vehicle ride. This angel took me home and stayed over to watch over me. I spent the night sitting up on a dining room chair with pillows piled high on the table in front of me. No way could I get into bed. The idea was for me to "sleep" this way for now. My daughter, who lived in Los Angeles, planned to get up early and drive to Las Vegas, to take over from my friend.

We'll figure this out, I said to myself.

Once Alexanne arrives, and through a referral from another friend, a doctor speaks to me on the phone and arranges for my daughter to go to his office to get a prescription for painkillers for me because the one given to me at the hospital was only a two-day supply. He also arranges for me to get an open MRI, so we'll know exactly what's going on with my back. Because of claustrophobia, I can't fathom the idea of being slid into the long tube of a regular MRI machine. Later, in the hospital, I'll be pressured into it anyway, so getting the open MRI ended up being an episode of agony with no return on investment.

In the whole Las Vegas Valley, at this time, there's only one, yes, one, open MRI machine. It's a twenty-minute drive, something I simply can't imagine enduring. Instinctually, it seems I shouldn't be doing this, but the doctor prescribed the painkillers on the promise that I'll get the MRI.

Later, doctors will tell me that all the movement involved in that car ride caused more damage to my back and will extend my recuperation.

In the end, it takes more than an hour to get there, and more than an hour to get me back home.

My ever-patient and lovable daughter has her own tale about that drive, something she's not about to forget: every small bump in the road reduced me to tears, to moaning, to pleading with her to slow down due to back spasms. She drives no more than five to ten miles per hour, slowing to a near-stop for speed bumps, any bumps, the car's emergency blinkers on the whole way.

The ride goes something like this.

"PLEASE slow down, oh my God, there's a bump coming, I see it!" Me.

"Mom? It's okay; I'm not hitting them on purpose. There's just so many! I can't avoid them all. What is it with this road?!" Her.

"Jesus H. Roosevelt Christ on a roasted cracker, THAT doesn't help," I say, anger rising, only to immediately deflate at the hopelessness of the situation.

I cannot believe it's me sitting in this car, my emotional nervous system shooting through the stratosphere with each spasm.

Every now and then we remember that ride together and chuckle at the memory. Isn't it so true that things we find awful in the moment sometimes end up being the source of our humor?

Once back home, the walk upstairs takes at least fifteen minutes. I repark myself on the dining room chair. Alexanne piles more pillows on the table in front of me, and packs some more on the back of the chair and on a chair next to me. From exhaustion and the painkiller I took on the ride over, while leaning ever so slightly forward with my head on those pillows, I sleep for a solid half hour. I will also later discover that, along with that car ride, sitting up like this also damaged my back further.

Instead of my getting better, the pain becomes increasingly difficult to handle. The strength of the spasms each time I move even a tenth of an inch, or when Alex touches me to help me to the bathroom, or to try to make me more comfortable, pushes me into an alternate reality where there is only pain. Everything else becomes its backdrop, like the stuff you hardly see during high-action fight scenes in movies.

The doctor calls with the MRI results: eight broken vertebrae confirmed. He wants me to go to his office. No way. The pain prescription, meant to just hold me over until things can be figured out, nearly runs out and the doctor won't renew it unless I see him. Alexanne, through connections, finds out she can buy me some on the street, but at an astronomical price.

"Mom, Mom, you *have* to go to the doctor. You have to!"

I stare into space, ignoring her.

In desperation, exhausted after looking after her idiot of a stubborn mother who insists she's fine despite sitting up in a chair for three days and nights, in excruciating pain, decides to call her brother. I'd wanted to wait for his vacation to be over before saying anything to him—no sense in disturbing his chill time with what's most certainly nothing. Ah.

We humans sure are good at believing any old story we tell ourselves.

It's after I ask her to hold a bowl between my legs for me to pee in because I can no longer attempt a walk to the bathroom that she calls Paul without telling me.

She still loves me, but I'm not sure how or why. I'm just grateful.

By then, though they seem to do nothing for the pain, the opioids—which have nearly run out—have taken me down into a place from which I won't resurface for six months. Think the scene in the movie *What Dreams May Come* when Robin Williams goes into hell to rescue his dead wife. He finds her there, but she seems to not understand where she is, and why he's there. After going through my own hell, I understand why she can hardly connect with him, her psyche now high above her body like a cloud, a shadow. It's because she finds herself unable to deal with her emotional pain. Mine's physical, but pain is pain.

While in that space, out of my foggy brain, I see my son standing just on the other side of the dining room table from me.

"Paul! What...what are you doing here?" I ask, certain he can't be there. Things aren't so bad that Alex called him. Are they? Would she betray me like that?

Imagine my shock when he answers me.

"I came to visit. Alex called. How do you feel?"

I stare dumbly, in shock over what I think is a drug-induced apparition answering me.

"You're really here?" I whisper, still suspicious, despite the confirmation of hearing his voice as clear as if he were really standing in front of me. Which he is.

"Yeah, I'm here." His eyes show concern, though his lips tremble some in the corners. "You can't just keep sitting there, you know," he adds.

I say nothing, my eyes glued to his as if our eyeballs are magnets; his positive, mine negative. In my peripheral vision, a part of me registers his sister standing just off to his left, arms crossed, the same look in her eyes, though her concern mixes with frustration after dealing with me on her own for several days.

I catch a look between them. *See, I told you; something's really wrong with Mom*, say my daughter's eyes. *I see what you mean*, say my son's.

I look down at the dining room table, or rather to the pile of pillows on it. If I say nothing, maybe they'll go away and leave me to swim in the swamp of what's become my mind. If I ignore the screaming of my back, the fact I've been sitting on the same chair for three days, and the fact of having to pee in a bowl, it's not all bad, really.

My son has been at my home less than thirty minutes when he calls EMTs despite my protests.

"I'll be fine; I'll heal. Our bodies heal themselves, you know," I mumble with less certainty than I might have in the past.

Soon, much like Paul, EMTs appear in the same spot I first saw him, their bags of tricks and an evacuation chair in tow.

"Maryse, we'll need to ask you a few questions to make sure you're coherent so we can take you."

Well, bless him in his innocence.

He asks my full name, date of birth, who the president is, and today's date. I'm the Queen of this Chair, born on a cold Tuesday morning, Mr. Nixon is about to quit his job, and today is the day I don't go to the hospital.

As I intended, after *that* answer, they refuse to take me.

I now can't believe that, even then, I still believed I'd be better in the morning...

These two beautiful and patient humans I gave birth to will later tell me that after I sent the people who could help me away, they huddled on the balcony of my condo with the door closed so I couldn't hear them. There, they conspire on how to get me as relaxed as possible with CBD and THC tinctures, so I'd allow the EMTs to take me to the hospital, where they strongly believe I belonged. Get Mom so high she won't complain about going off in an ambulance, they reason.

Later, I'll discover that Paul gave me several droppers full of CBD along with only half a dropper of THC—he wants me relaxed, but not high. He knows THC makes me paranoid.

It works.

The EMTs return and this time I answer their questions. Reluctantly, but also correctly. There follows an awful descent of the staircase in my condo, me strapped to an evacuation chair into which I somehow got myself. With my eyes closed and face scrunched up, holding my breath, the two EMTs hold me and the chair above their heads to clear a narrow ninety-degree angle at the landing. An ambulance ride I wish to forget follows, me having to move myself from that chair and onto the gurney since I won't let them touch me. It takes a solid five minutes.

Once at the hospital, to my vehement protests—I want to remain on the ambulance gurney to avoid the pain that awaits me if I move—the staff at the hospital joins ranks with the EMTs to convince me to move onto the emergency room bed so the EMTs can have their gurney back.

Of course, no way do I allow anyone to help. That would smash the dinger on my pain-o-meter, which, in my mind, resembles that old-time carnival game where a big-armed guy in a wifebeater shirt hits a piece of wood on the ground that magically sends a dinger up a rail in the center of a post, at the top of which is a large, gold, circle-shaped bell. If he hits it hard enough, the dinger hits the bell, and he wins a stuffed rabbit. Or a teddy bear. Anyway, my dinger smashes to smithereens anytime it hits the bell, and it hits it at least three times per hour, sometimes more. And I don't even get a teddy bear!

Once I'm on the emergency room bed, I'm told that the doctor is admitting me to the hospital. The staff once again wants me to move to a gurney so they can transport me to my assigned room. I'll then have to move from the gurney to the hospital bed. But, I've had it. No more moving. No way. I refuse.

In the end, they wheel me to my room in the emergency room bed and leave me in it. I'm sure that, after they get me settled, once outside my room, they'll roll their eyes and run away and hope I'm gone by their next shift. It's what I'd do. Yet, that doesn't happen. Instead, they show remarkable patience and kindness whenever they deal with me.

Several days passed before the nurses manage to convince me to let them move me onto the more comfortable regular room bed. They say it's better for my back. They say they can simply slide me onto it by placing the beds right next to each other and transferring me from bed to bed by pulling on the sheet underneath me. My body will, of course, follow.

And, as Elton John once sang, *I'm high as a kite by then*, except in my case, I'm not in space, but on opioids and muscle relaxers, and better able to manage it despite the still-excruciating pain.

Doomed

A week into my stay at that first hospital, my body and mind now drenched in drugs, I lie, listless in my bed, staring at the white wall in front of me, not daring to move.

The door to my room opens and my eyes travel to it. A doctor I've never seen before comes in. He stands at the foot of my bed, a lookalike of Dr. "McDreamy" on *Grey's Anatomy*, but thirty years older, hands in the pockets of his white coat, face grim. Without introducing himself—so busy that he doesn't have time for such courtesies—he goes right into what he's come to say.

"All the tests are back. You have multiple myeloma..." He trails off, looking at me expectantly.

I stare at him, confused. I have what, now? Is he talking about me?

"What's that?" I ask, poking my nose above my opioid cloud, vaguely curious.

He looks at me as if he doesn't really want to say, as if I should know. You'd think instinct would have kicked in by now, that I'd feel something: fear, deeper curiosity, a desire to know. But no. Firmly ensconced in the cocoon of the various medications running through my body, I remain oblivious. Calm. Mildly interested only. Half of my mind on when my son will get here with the smoothie he promised me. That's about all I "eat" now. My appetite's left me much like birds leave in the winter. And it's winter in my life.

He sighs, keeps looking at me. I blink, twice. His hesitation causes me to become more engaged with what he's trying to say. What could be so bad that he can't get the words out?

"It's a cancer of plasma cells. In the bone marrow." Not *your* bone marrow, mind you, but *the* bone marrow. As if to distance me from it. As if he could.

The door to my room swings opens, sounds from the corridor rush in; a blast of cooler air, the faint dings of faraway medical equipment, an announcement over the speaker system, people walking by in conversation, normal hospital noises. A nurse's head pops in. When she sees the doctor, she says she'll come back later.

Meanwhile, the doc and I continue our staring contest—he, still at the foot of my bed. Why isn't he saying it's going to be okay, that it can be fixed?

"Well...what does that mean...? What do I do?"

"You'll have to see an oncologist for treatment," he replies. I can see his hands moving in his pockets as if playing with something in there, a pen perhaps, a coin, his keys, or maybe he's just twitchy that way.

"But. What is it? Why do I have it?" I continue. I become conscious of my heart beating ever so much faster than two minutes ago.

"We don't know why people get it. It's incurable," he says quickly, like one afraid he won't get the words out unless he blurts them.

Incurable?

Is he serious? Who is he? What's he doin' in my room telling me this!

Without taking my eyes off his, my right hand crawls toward the bed control remote. I press the button that will raise the back of the bed so I can see him better. Whir goes the mechanism.

"What do you mean, incurable?" I ask. "Why do I have this? Are you sure?"

"Yes, we're sure. We conducted many tests and the results are all the same," he says, now shifting from one leg to the other. Maybe he's tired of this conversation; maybe he's nervous.

"But if it's not curable, how long... I mean...am I going to die?"

I hold my breath.

Scrutinize his face for the answer.

You know, the one I *want* to hear. Where he looks confused for a minute, but then laughs and says, "No, not at all! We have a pill for that now!"

Instead, his eyes grow larger, his mouth opens, then closes.

My eyes remain fixed on his. A flutter develops in my chest.

Finally, "People who have it typically live three to five years after diagnosis."

My eyes on him grow larger; the flutter expands.

"I'm sorry," he adds.

But he just looks like he can't wait to get out of my room.

And to think. I've been consumed by the fact I can barely move, sit, stand up, or walk.

That my back is broken.

It seems I've worried about something that doesn't even matter.

I mean, what's the point of being able to walk again if I'll be dead soon?

PART II

CHAOS

There is Fuckery Afoot

Okay, Guy Ritchie, yes, I did steal the title of this chapter from the script for *The Gentlemen*, but hey, I couldn't help myself. It's what you get for using such a *fantastical* phrase. I love it too much to remove it. Unless you sue me, but please don't. In any case, you took the expression from somewhere other than your imagination based on my internet research (clearing my throat here). Anyway, thank you for bringing it to my attention.

The phrase has come to mind because, to its credit, the fuckery that unleashed on my life attempted to make itself known, to give me warning it was headed my way, that it was there. It became insistent about a month before The Event, but even years ahead of that, signs appeared.

The only reason I felt compelled to ignore the signs must be that The Event and what followed were a necessary life lesson for me. If you believe in that stuff, more than one palm reader has pointed out that my lifeline is split in two; in palmistry, a split lifeline indicates that a tragic event will occur, but that life will go on afterward. Coincidence?

Prior to breaking my back, during my many weekly walks on a local park trail, I sensed something afoot; my body felt different, my left hip acting a bit wonky, for instance. The real pain started during my first few days in San Miguel de Allende, Mexico, where I'd gone for a writer's conference. I strolled on quaint cobblestone streets between the hotel where the conference took place and the house I'd rented for the duration, just two short blocks away. As I walked, which had become painful, I found it difficult to appreciate the bougainvillea framing ancient doors and window frames on vibrant yellow, ocher, and sometimes dusty pink houses.

On Day Three, because I didn't want pain to distract me during workshops, I began to swallow anything over the counter I could get my hands on to control it: me, the one with the world summits in her head over the taking of even just an aspirin.

Big red flag right there! No, a balloon, a blimp! The Goodyear Blimp, floating about my life, filled with warnings instead of helium.

Later, once home from the hospital for nearly a year, no longer using a walker and rarely wearing a back brace, but still struggling with movement, I'm on a video call with my daughter.

She surprises me by saying that she thinks it's a generation-wide issue; baby boomers don't address issues head on. We ignore them. We hope they'll resolve themselves. As if. Apparently, we look at that proverbial hole in the sidewalk and fall into it. Every time. We never simply walk around it, according to her.

In other words, we see imminent fuckery but do nothing? I hope she's wrong, but is that not exactly what *I* did?

My self-allotted weekly glass of red Bordeaux clinks as I put it down on my stone coffee table. I nearly miss because I'm staring at her on my screen, unable to think of what to say to that because of my secret.

I've had several mystical experiences throughout my life, some where I've been guided by I-don't-know-what to go in a certain direction or do certain things that later turned out to be right for me. And some seemed on the surface to have no purpose at all. Not even years later can I say a purpose presented itself. But I also now know that even with these no-purpose events, things were most likely working below the surface to change something, to warn me, save me, redirect me.

A few years ago, I visited a small town in Arizona and had lunch on the patio of a restaurant located in a golf course community. The patio faced the green.

Imagine yourself sitting on that patio for the first time, two friends with you, everyone drinking Don Julio Añejo margaritas. You're all nearly at the bottom of the second one when, out of the corner of your left eye, you notice a few cows "out there." It takes you a few seconds to process that it's a golf course there on your left, not a field. You whip your head that way and scrutinize the scene.

Hey, look at that, you say to your friends. They turn in unison to follow your gaze. You all stare at the cows. No one says a word at first. You glance at your margaritas, at each other, then back at the cows, and suddenly, one of you says—*moi*, in this case—*holy shit! There's cows on the golf course!* I'd later discover that, though not visible from a distance, a wire fence and shrubbery separate the cows' area from the fairway, but on that day, we assumed that the cows grazed on the course.

How can you not love a place that gives you the impression that cows hang out on the golf course?

So, of course, I bought a house there. What fun to live in a place where people found a way to mix golfing and cows on the same piece of land. What other exciting things might happen here? My compulsion to buy the house eclipsed reason.

I already owned a home in Las Vegas at the time and didn't need a second home in the countryside of Arizona, twenty minutes from the Nogales border with Mexico. Or another mortgage. A seemingly stupid move since, at the time, I found myself between projects and had no income at all, just savings. Yet, eighteen months later, when real estate prices were frantically clawing their way into the stratosphere like mice on speed, I sold that house and made enough of a profit to take a four-year vacation.

Many years after the house had been sold, a famous psychic I was gifted to a session with called me an *incompetent competent*. She explained it as an ability to do a right thing for myself without realizing why I was doing it at the time. So, this explained how I'd come to buy that house when I didn't understand why I was buying it at the time I bought it. I know, that's a lot of purchases in one sentence.

Years before that, I stood at the kitchen sink washing dishes at my home in Las Vegas. I heard my mother call my name in an urgent way as clearly as if she stood next to me. My head whipped around, and I scanned the whole kitchen, confused. She was more than 2,500 miles away in Montreal at the time, not here at my house. Startled, I stopped washing a pot halfway through and called my childhood home where my father and she still lived together.

My younger brother answered and told me that our mother was at the hospital with our father, who'd suffered a mild heart attack and had been taken there by ambulance. My lovingly odd bird of a brother wasn't one to take the initiative to call and share such news, or any news, so had I not heard my mother's voice, I probably wouldn't have known about my father's heart attack for several days until mother got around to calling.

In 1994, after months of thinking about it daily, I made an appointment and went to my favorite plastic surgeon, and told him something wasn't right, that he should remove the breast implants he'd put in me a little more than a year back. Luckily, he took my "something isn't right" seriously, examined me, and found a lump, then sent me for the usual tests. The diagnosis came back as Stage I of a rare breast cancer.

Had I not had that strong niggling feeling, who knows when I might have discovered that cancer. Since women still regularly died of breast cancer at the time—they still do, I know, but not at as great a rate—I might not have lived to get cancer again years later, to change my life, to tell this story.

While living in New York City in my early twenties, I'd read an instruction book on out-of-body experiences and began to meditate in a way that might bring one on for me. I wanted the mystical experience. Every day, I worked at it for thirty minutes, sometimes more.

About a month in, while lying on the bed, feeling frustrated because my mind hadn't yet left my body, I asked myself, "Why can't I do this? I'm doing everything the book says to do!"

At the same moment, it dawned on me that I had thought that while looking down at my body from the ceiling on the opposite corner of the room. When the realization hit me, my consciousness tumbled back down into my body, which jolted and propelled me right out of bed and onto the floor.

So. Why did I not get a warning that a health crisis of the magnitude I experienced was headed my way with the force of an asteroid in a science fiction movie? I told everyone it hit me—whack—right out of the blue.

But if I were Pinocchio, my nose would have grown by six inches each time I said it.

You see, circa 2006, while I lived in the house I bought in Arizona because of the cows on the golf course, I had a breast thermography scan, something I did every two years since my breast cancer diagnosis. This time, the provider offered me an extra scan that would cover my whole torso instead of just my breasts. I said yes.

The results came back negative on the breasts, but the therapist showed me where the thermography had picked up areas of strong inflammation elsewhere in my torso, especially in my back—*areas where in 2018 it would be shown the multiple myeloma mostly resided.*

In case you don't know, thermography picks up inflammation in the body years before anything manifests in the form of, say, tumors, or other forms of cancer. If you worry about breast cancer, for instance, get thermography regularly, and you'll know eons before a tumor is formed, when you can still fix it without surgery and chemo.

So, that day, the therapist urged me to call the doctor who'd read the scan because he wanted to discuss the results with me.

Something about it frightened me, and except for when I went to the plastic surgeon because of a feeling, I still had a propensity to look away, way away. And to pretend that what scared me didn't exist. So, in full ostrich mode, I never called that doctor.

Looking back, I find it difficult to not think this disease was meant to be for the lessons it taught me.

Instead, I completely ignored, buried, and stomped on any thoughts of those results when they occasionally resurfaced from the depth of my psyche, like whales leaping up above the surface before flopping back down into the deep, the way deep.

I never had thermography again.

Which means that for twelve years, this thing festered in me. Which means I could have stopped it early. Which means I could have avoided a broken back.

Then, beginning a few months before The Event, some things started to manifest in my body. An instinctual desire to go get a full physical tickled at my mind, but it scared me, so down went my head into the proverbial sand.

I wanted to find out why my left hip now hurt after my several weekly walks. Why I was now out of breath after climbing the stairs to my condo whereas I'd usually climb them like a mountaineer at the halfway point to Everest. Why I often felt too tired to go out, either forcing myself or giving up and going to bed too early.

All out of character for me. I promised myself I'd make the call.

But I'd booked myself into that writer's conference in Mexico. I'd wanted to attend for many years and something in me must have known I'd cancel if I knew.

So, of course, I ignored the signs. Repeat after *moi*: *I will never see the signs and ignore the signs.*

During the conference, the pain got so bad that the over-the-counter stuff no longer worked. I accepted strong painkillers a friend who lived there gave me once we'd met up near the end of the conference. They helped some and I kept on walking, though cutting it down a lot because I believed that the cobblestoned streets of San Miguel de Allende and Guanajuato were what had caused my increased pain since I'd arrived. I'd later discover that walking on cobblestones is a good thing for the body—unless your vertebrae happen to be on the verge of collapse, that is.

True fuckery.

Now in a hospital bed, dealing with the pain and learning to sit up and walk again still sidelines the bigger issue of the incurable cancer, at the last stages of which I find myself. I know...

But isn't it always the louder, most painful thing that lassos our attention when it comes to health?

Still, I know something must be done. The medical staff around me all talk as if some sort of chemo's a given for me. I don't argue but know there's no way that poison will be infused into my pretty little veins. Nope. *No way at all.*

I still feel convinced there's a better way to deal with it all, even if I don't know yet what that is.

This fuckery will eventually compel me to deal with it as one might deal with sour lemons, except I'll vow that it won't just be turned into lemonade, but into full-blown marmalade. I mean, if you're gonna turn something bad into something good, might as well keep some of the zing while you sweeten it up! Yin and yang and all that.

But it will take me more than a year to get there, a year of huge chaos with not even a faint halo of light to be seen around it.

From Tofu to Cherry Garcia

"What has been the point of me trying to eat so healthy all these years? Why did I spend all that money on organic this and that? I've tried to keep my weight down, read ingredient lists, didn't eat meat with hormones and antibiotics, my kitchen is nothing but healthy foods, no junk in sight. I ate the least offensive, preservative- and pesticides-wise, in restaurants. What was the point of all that?!" I ask-yell the tall, droopy-eyed doctor with a mop of dark brown curls falling to his collar and standing at the foot of my bed at the rehab hospital.

Even as tears fall down my face, I go on: "I'm still lying here in this bed with all these other people who probably ate *garbage* their whole lives!" I say, waving my arm toward the hallway and the other rooms—which brings on a back spasm, which makes me cringe in pain. Punishment for being unkind.

"Why after all that did *I* get sick just like them?"

The doctor looks forlorn. After a couple of false starts, he answers.

"I don't know. We never know about these things. All you can do is your best so you can walk again, so you can go home. You want to go home, right?"

I stare at "my" tree outside the window, something I do a lot. Too drugged out to read a book for very long, or to follow the plot of a movie, I mostly stare. At the tree. At the wall, at my legs, stretched out on the bed, useless.

"The only way we can release you is if you stand up, and if you're at least beginning to walk. Even if you just take two or three steps with your walker. Then, you can go home again," he says, offering this to me like a gift. All I see are the strings attached to it.

He's ignoring the whole food thing, taking me back to the issue of walking instead.

Except.

The next day—not his usual day for seeing me—he shows up, out of breath like he's been walking fast or running, at the foot of my bed and says, "I thought about your question last night; it kept me up half the night." He looks happy about it; giddy, even.

I can't hide my surprise; sure it shows on my face. He continues: "We're not taught about nutrition in medical school, not told that it can make a difference, okay? But, because of my wife and because I'm interested too, we eat really healthy. Like you, we eat clean, mostly organic, grass-fed meats only, and we pay attention to the new science that has to do with nutrition. And we read labels."

Not knowing what to say, I wait, curious about this turn of events, about his admission that doctors get no nutritional training. I know that, but they usually don't say.

"The difference between you and them," he says, pointing toward the hallway, "is that I'm pretty sure you're the only person here who only has the one issue to deal with..."

I open my mouth to say something, but he puts up a hand like a stop sign and continues. "Even if it's a doozy you're dealing with. Imagine if you had diabetes, or if you were obese, or if you had heart problems on top of a broken back—which will heal—and an incurable cancer?"

Like that's nothing?

I shrug, gaze out the window at the tree.

"So, even though you're dealing with that, keep going with taking care of your health in any way you can. It makes a difference."

"Okay," I say in a near whisper, uninterested, the thought that I'd done that for most of my adulthood in mind, yet it hadn't saved me. Diabetes and heart troubles are controllable, much more so than an incurable cancer deep in the marrow of one's bones. I don't add that I've been a firm believer that my ninety-percent clean diet would keep me healthy forever. And yet, clearly it hasn't.

"Well, I have to go. I have rounds in the other building but promise me you'll keep it up."

He makes to leave, but pauses, waiting for my answer.

"Okay, I will," I say, wanting to make him feel good about going out of his way to come tell me that.

Thank you, dear doctor *whose-name-I've-forgotten*, for attempting to lift my heart, but I don't believe you.

Because I can't stop wondering... if cancer found me despite my mostly health freak ways, my so-called clean diet, why bother eating healthy? Really? Why did *I* have cancer, and not my four eat-all-the-junk-I-can-get-down siblings?

And then it emerges from the depths of my mind. Despite all my soapbox elegies about eating healthy, I have a secret. I've often said that the addiction gene passed me by, but that's not entirely true.

I'm addicted to a legal drug that's in practically everything we eat: sugar. And my "reward foods" at this point typically mean something with sugar.

According to the alternative side of the medical fence, sugar is cancer's rocket fuel.[1]

But those on the mainstream side of the same fence deny this by saying (correctly) that all our cells need sugar. However, they follow this up by stating that it *can* indirectly contribute to causing cancer and its growth; it occurs from the relationship

---

1. https://sciforschenonline.org/journals/cancer-research/article-data/IJCRMM-2-127/IJCRMM-2-127.pdf   and https://beatcancer.org/blog/more-on-sugar-and-cancer/

between cancer and insulin resistance and insulin-like growth factors in the blood. This can cause weight gain which increases our risk of diabetes and heart disease. It is also a proven risk factor in thirteen different kinds of cancer. One of which is multiple myeloma.[2]

So, really what they're saying is that sugar *does* affect outcome in cancer, just not directly. Well, if I take the long way 'round back to my house, I still get home, right?

I've known that overconsumption of sugar isn't any good for overall health. Sugary foods have zero nutritional reward and an overload of calories. It causes us to gain weight because excess sugar in the body gets converted into fatty acids and stored as body fat. Without going all medical jargon on you, in the end, excess weight increases the risk of developing type 2 diabetes (runs in my family) and heart disease (that too). Also, obesity has been linked to multiple myeloma in studies, which might not have included people just somewhat overweight like me, who carried about ten more pounds than necessary for twenty years before diagnosis. What if there's a connection there, too?

But—even after a breast cancer diagnosis many years back—one cancer that even the conventional side says might be affected by sugar[3] —I've allowed myself to fall for it, over and

---

2. https://connect.mayoclinic.org/blog/cancer-education-center/newsfeed-post/sugars-role-in-cancer/ and https://www.oncologynutrition.org/erfc/healthy-nutrition-now/sugar-and-cancer

3. https://www.webmd.com/breast-cancer/features/sugar-and-breast-cancer

over. To "reward" myself with it when I'd been good for a while. My kryptonite.

At this point, convinced that it's the sugar and nothing but the sugar that did it, I resolve to delve into ways to consciously combat the addiction. Usually, I think about eating sugary foods for a day or so before succumbing, and when I do, in go the danged sugar-laden foods, followed by feelings of guilt for hours and days afterward, further damaging my body with those punishing emotions. Unproductive to the max.

While still in rehab, and even after my conversation with *Dr. Eat Organic*, and not clear-headed at all, I start searching the internet for ways to overcome a sugar addiction. And follow that up with searches for "cancer diets"—many of which say to stop eating all sugar, even fruit.

I find hundreds, perhaps thousands of testimonials from people who claim to have been cured of cancer by just changing their diets.

Would it work for me?

I look for commonalties, for studies on their validity, and end up more confused than ever about nutrition. About sugar.

I lose my mind.

I chuck it all out, ignore all the research.

Once home from the hospital, I'll go rogue and return to my routine of mostly eating clean, caving into cravings, feeling guilty about it, and returning to eating well.

But something will compel me to do it differently this time. I'll pay attention to myself as I eat that pint of Cherry Garcia, act as an observer.

Also, I'll accept the guilt that comes afterward, focus on it until it dissipates, rather than trying to force it away.

A Buddhist monk once taught me that neat trick. You just have to use it for it to work. Just thinking about it does nothing, something I sometimes forget (said with tongue in cheek).

It's a way to dissolve a negative or painful feeling. He told me to laser-focus on the part of my body where the feeling is making itself known until I no longer feel it. It can take up to thirty seconds for the change to take place, but, yes, the negative feelings I've focused on in this way have all dissipated. It feels as if the feeling is evaporating like a shallow water puddle under a bright sun.

So, the cravings lessen. It's as if once I give myself permission to enjoy the foods I crave, no matter how devoid of nutrition the calories might be, I don't want them nearly as much.

Later, my research will lead me to understand that sugar isn't such a demon that I should stop eating anything that turns to sugar in my body. Its consumption calls for moderation and for getting it from sources that offer some nutrition along with it, like fiber, minerals, and antioxidants, such as found in fruit.

Still, things keep getting in the way of my healing journey, as if the Universe wants to test my resolve.

My parents passed away ten years before my diagnosis; my father at age eighty-five, my mother at age eighty-seven. Until their early eighties they enjoyed decent health. They then declined over a period of about four or five years, and both passed away from illness.

On the same day, nine hours apart. Yup.

They ate a typical Western diet. My four siblings? They eat that same way. None of them have had any health issues of the magnitude I've faced. At least, not yet.

My sister hadn't graced any kind of doctor's office in more than twenty years at the time of my diagnosis, which scared her into doing a full checkup. She kept the testing and the results from me until a year later when we happened to enter a conversation about medical testing.

She smokes three packs of cigarettes a day (she's been a smoker for fifty-three years), is sixty pounds overweight (at least), and eats whatever she wants, whenever she wants. She also drinks about two cocktails each time she goes out to dinner, which is two to three times per week.

My brothers? Same thing. Though none of them smoke and they're not overweight, they eat junk, never read food labels, and have no interest in doing so.

One thing my siblings seem to share is an ability to let disturbing things flow away from them; they don't linger on the bad stuff. As the oversensitive one in the family, in the past, I've allowed said bad stuff to cling to me like to the sticky side of Velcro.

When my sister tells me about the tests and their results, it topples my emotional state like dominoes.

Anger. Depression. Hopelessness. *Clack, clack, clack.*

I want to ignore medical treatment, healthy diet, meditation, Chinese herbs, supplements, keeping a calm state of mind, everything and anything I've been trying on to get well.

You see, her diagnostic tests all came back...negative. As in no sign of any disease anywhere in her body.

Yet I, the official family health freak...have cancer. Again.

Why? I want to cry, scream, kill something, and not necessarily in that order.

After her revelation, though internally this time, I resume the screaming fit I had at the rehab hospital in front of *Dr. Eat Organic*. Fuck eating organic fruits and vegetables, and grass-fed meat, and only wild Alaskan salmon when it comes to fish. It has served me not at all.

Yet, I really believe in Hippocrates's "Let food be thy medicine and medicine be thy food." So, of course, my mind keeps returning to it even after my tantrums. Maniacally almost, I still buy mainly healthy food despite my erratic thoughts on the subject.

I ignore the fact that I sneak in "reward food" nearly daily, so no matter how clean I eat the rest of the day, eating a half bag of red licorice or other candy while watching a movie at night nearly completely negates how good I've been all day. After *rewarding* myself, I feel guilty, of course, adding yet more negative energy to my overwhelmed emotional body.

It took the loud siren of multiple myeloma more than two years to cure me of my nearly daily reward food habit. It's not a reward at all if it contributes to you ending up with a broken back, and in an infusion room full of people on chemo drips. And you're one of them.

Meanwhile, I need something else.

Or something more.

Some help. I need help.

Guru Hopping

There's a war raging on in the United States. I don't mean the one between Republicans and Democrats. I mean the one between Team Pro Big Pharma (chemotherapy, proteasome inhibitors, monoclonal antibodies, immunotherapy, etc.) and Team I-Healed-My-Cancer-With-This-Alternative-Treatment (insert alternative of choice). This war rages on with other diseases, too, but the one related to cancer concerns me most, obviously.

And it's not pretty, let me tell you. If you think you might enjoy becoming completely confused about the best way to treat cancer, any cancer, just spend an hour or two online reading articles from each team.

You might find the insults hurled from one to the other—like hockey pucks sent flying across the ice at warp speed by hyped-up hockey players—entertaining. At least, until, like me, you realize that this slinging of factoids gets you nowhere near the healing you seek. Watching a movie about some hero saving the world does nothing to save your world. Watching this war offers little in the way of real solutions.

Most of all, you end up confused. Frustrated. Left at a loss as to what the right thing to do might be; you can't reach out to the experts because the experts are busying themselves with the above-mentioned war. Each side points shaking-from-rage fingers at the other.

"Big Pharma is killing us all in the name of profits!" says Team Pro Alternatives.

"All these quacks just want your money, and don't care if you die!" says Team Pro Big Pharma.

After *Dr. Keep-Eating-Organic* leaves my room, I gaze at my tree while I think about my condition, about what he said. And think some more, until a switch inside me flips.

I don't have many conscious, lucid minutes because of the drugs, but this day, despite my discouraged state of mind, I resolve to keep digging online for answers. Surely, *something* can be done about this prognosis, this awful situation. Somewhere in the ether, a cure *must* exist. One that preferably doesn't include infusions of anything resembling chemotherapy drugs—which, at this time, I still equate to death itself.

My searches will be conducted with an open mind, I resolve. I'll check out how doctors, allopathic and alternative, in other countries treat patients with multiple myeloma. Read up on all the possible cures, check out the source, see what testing has been done, if any, and without that, how much anecdotal evidence exists for any treatment I consider. I'll find a commonality between them. I will!

I bury myself into all manner of alternative treatment research, and into what the conventional team has to say about it. One could argue it serves as a distraction from the devastating diagnosis I face.

Months pass. I'm off the strong meds now, and my confusion meter goes into the red thinking back to those opioid-addled days searching the web for alternative and holistic treatments to avoid Big Pharma pharmacopeia and to, hopefully, find a cure.

The one I've been told time and again doesn't exist.

We've all experienced the zombie state we enter when going down an internet funnel, which feels like being in a raft on a tortuous, downhill lazy river at a water park. *Oooh*, look at what Beyoncé ate last night! And would you believe what Celine Dion looks like now? Megan Fox stopped talking to Jennifer Aniston; why?

Click Here to Find Out!

Click Here!

Click Here!

Click HERE!

That's entertainment for you, folks. You might think I've gone down *this* twisting lazy river, but I next to never read online gossip, especially when it comes to celebrities. I consider it a time suck of fantasy tales. There's enough fantasy in my own mind, and turmoil in my world, without adding to it.

Then, the conspiracy stuff. An alien ship landed in this woman's backyard last night and she's not been the same since. *Really?* The Bush family is from a reptilian alien race that came to Earth to take it over, but then this other alien race came too, and they've been battling for control ever since. Kinda like Republicans versus Democrats.

No, my lazy river of choice is the one I choose to believe will present me with the danged nonexistent cure, dammit. So I won't have to do "those drugs," more dammit. And so I'll be healed, or at least in remission the rest of my life. Dammit.

Getting out of that raft takes…what *does* it take?

For me, it only takes a complete meltdown. Which most likely occurs because of my expectation that my health situation will resolve itself by the sheer force of me expecting it to do just that.

I begin my research by looking for alternative cancer treatments since I've been told that even no kind of chemo will put this baby down for good. Ah…the stuff on offer out there as the end-all cure-all for cancer, any cancer, all cancers!

From swallowing toxic chemicals in small amounts, to fasting for weeks, to eating only pounds and pounds of beets every day until the cancer is gone, it's out there.

Gurus abound.

People say they cured themselves of cancer by simply changing their diets to vegan (no animal protein). Or paleo (lots of animal protein). Some swear by vegetables only, others by meat only, fruit only, fish only, chocolate only, THC only, and it goes on ad infinitum. And right on their tails, like lions after antelopes, are those who verbally crucify them for making those claims.

Both sides argue their case well.

One can't help but wonder: Why are entire websites dedicated to bringing down people who say this or that cured them? What's in it for the "reviewer" to spend what surely takes days to write in depth about individuals who profess to have been cured of cancer by following a certain protocol not sanctioned by Team Pro Big Pharma?

What's up with them dedicating this much time and energy putting out multiple-page reports to discredit the "healed"?

Who pays for this?

Then, there's the clinics. Worldwide, there are clinics whose marketing shouts out all manner of cures for cancer. Many such clinics can be found in Mexico, especially in Tijuana, a hub of alternative treatment clinics for all types of ailments, as well as for antiaging and injectables to plump up lips, cheeks, even your other cheeks. But, in my research, I found that most of these clinics stick to the highly profitable cancer industry.

Many of the patients who find their way to them have been sent home to die by their American, Canadian, or European oncologists. But, to some, it's a first step. Do this and if it doesn't work, try chemo. Which makes sense. You don't take a car engine apart until after you've tried to fix it by changing this or that part—you know, the least damaging stuff first.

A plan begins to form in my head. I'll go to this clinic as soon as my back heals enough for me to make the journey. I estimate another three or four months. During this time, I continue to dig online for answers, though I initiate contact with what seems to be the most reputable clinic among them. I even get to talk to a patient with multiple myeloma who has gone there and has had good results (though she will later switch to allopathic treatment due to both the expense and the not-good-*enough* results).

What can they do to reverse this awful thing swimming about like dwarf lantern sharks in the marrow of my bones?

They tell me what I want to hear: that what my American oncologists mean when they say death comes to multiple myeloma patients within three to five years is that this is the longest amount of time chemo can keep me alive. *Their* treatments, however, will keep me alive forever.

Just the jam I'm looking for.

You'll find similar clinics in Thailand, South America, in pretty much any country where regulations aren't as strict as in the United States, Canada, and the European Union.

Most of the treatments they offer have never gone through clinical trials because, from a Big Pharma company's point of view—the only ones with pockets deep enough to pay for such trials—there's not enough money to be made from these types of natural treatments. The clinics show a plethora of anecdotal evidence, all from their own patients. I'm skeptical.

A patient runs into four obstacles when considering entering these clinics.

Cost.

Scammers.

Wasting time on treatments that don't work while not pursuing those that do.

Possibly dying because of it.

What I will only find out much later is that they neglected to tell me that, with good and proven alternative treatments *in addition* to chemo and its cousins—East and West hand in hand—I stand a greater chance of going into permanent remission. Of possibly being cured. It will be more than a year before I make this discovery, a year of what was near complete chaos in my healthcare.

The clinic I consider in Mexico wants $60,000 for a two-week stay, but they recommend three weeks for me. In return, they'll feed me an all-organic diet free of meat, gluten, and dairy. I'll get two or three alternative treatments per day. When I see that, I realize I'm in the wrong business. I mean, the profit margins must be 1,000 percent or more. Apparently, the fact that the treatments themselves don't cost that much doesn't mean the clinic will pass along the discount. It's difficult not to feel that there's a gouging of desperate people going on.

Meanwhile, I enroll in online classes that teach how to heal cancer holistically, read the blogs of cancer survivors and explore the cures they used, join online multiple myeloma groups, read information on our gov's health websites, dig up experts.

Ah, the experts... what can one say about them?

I research one expert after another, one guru after the next from Team I-Healed-My-Cancer-With-This-Alternative-Treatment.

One such *guru*, a man stricken with the dreaded Big C in his twenties, claims to have healed his Stage III colon cancer though nutrition only, no chemo, ten years before he appears on my computer monitor. But, when you dig deeper, you discover that before his nutritional crusade began, a surgeon removed his tumor. He just didn't do any chemo afterward, which had been highly recommended to him.

For the *sin* of having had his tumor removed before he turned his diet, and most likely his life, upside down, one of those aforementioned "reviewers" took the time to write a long exposé rife with references to the guru's website. He included videos (which the reviewer most likely stole from our guru's YouTube channel) throughout the review in which the young man talks about how he cured his own cancer through diet alone. If I were to write such an exposé myself, it would take me a week, at least, to gather all that *evidence*, write the article, go find the videos, and put the whole thing together.

Why would someone go through the trouble? I ask myself.

What's in it for this doctor reviewer? Surely, it's not just his Western medical training ego that made him want to do this.

As for our guy who healed his own cancer *with diet only*, as he does say often, why does he slam the chemo team, and any conventional treatments, as if he has something to lose if they succeed?

Could it not be that the surgery to remove his tumor *in combination* with the drastic diet change put him in full remission? Cured him?

Why don't these teams work together toward their common aim of curing cancer?

Where's the respect for the accomplishments of each?

In the end, I come to realize that none of the experts agree on anything, even those on the same side of the fence from which they make their argument. For every respected expert who says, "Do A! Don't do B!," I find another equally respectable expert who shouts out, "Do B! Don't do A!"

When I find out—from reading a letter written to a health blog by oncologist Dr. Peter Eisenberg—that oncologists make the largest share of their income, about seventy percent, from *selling chemo drugs to their patients*, I give up. If this isn't the hugest conflict of interest ever, I don't know what is.

To note, this doctor has dedicated much of his career to changing things so that doctors can make a living without relying on selling drugs or other unneeded services and treatments that don't suit their patients. The letter was posted in January 2009, and yet, here we are in 2022 (at the time of this writing) and doctors must still make a profit from add-ons to patient visits because health insurance companies do not reimburse them enough for those visits to keep their doors open.[1]

Because all of this makes me feel despondent and helpless with no solution in sight, I fall to eating foods I haven't eaten in years. Foods with preservatives, additives, and sugar, always sugar, my personal *épée de Damoclès*.

I've reached the point of TMI, too much information—firmly planted on the fence between the two teams. On which side should I fall?

And then, a fleeting thought...what if...what if I did away with the fence instead?

The thought remains hazy at best, something floating about on the other side of a badly warped windowpane.

One day, once again frustrated by the conflicting information Dr. Google presents to me, I chuck my laptop clear across my bedroom. Well, that's my intent, but still weak, and too fearful of back spasms, I watch it land on the edge of the foot of my bed, where I'm lying. It teeters there for a count of four before gliding down my duvet and onto the carpeted floor. I give it my best dirty look even though I can't see it from where I'm propped up against the headboard. I can't even manage to get something to fly beyond the edge of my bed...

I'm still at the bottom of the ocean fighting my way to the surface.

---

1. https://healthbeatblog.com/2009/01/a-very-open-letter-from-an-oncologist / , https://www.marincancercare.com/our-physicians/peter-eisenberg/

A nugget about the fence begins to form deep in my psyche that day, but I'll only notice it much later.

Meanwhile, fuck gurus.

So Many Tears, So Little Time

On the day I receive my diagnosis, in shock, I travel a gamut of emotions. I cry. Panic. Curl in on myself (in my head only, my broken body incapable of curling). I find myself nearly unable to handle the tsunami of despair that would consume me, were it not for the opioid haze surrounding it.

I wonder about the unfairness of it all. Why me, the health freak in my family? Why me, the one who never takes prescription drugs without first holding a summit with myself about it? Why me, the one who checks every food label and even researches some ingredients in depth before consuming a product?

That day, my children are notified.

They come. One from Dallas, the other from Los Angeles, both having decamped back to their respective homes after The

Event, both having tried to resume their working lives as much as one can when uncertainty waits in the corridor.

We cry.

We update my living trust.

A day later, Alexanne sits next to my hospital bed, holding my right hand.

"Now," I say, "you can either have the Henredon couch or the painting; not both."

I stare at her until she looks back at me. She's got the skill to sell ice to people who live in winter year-round, and I want her brother, my son, who'd give her anything, to have at least one of these two among my most-prized possessions. They once good-naturedly argued over which of them should get that down-filled couch if something happened to me, never thinking it would ever be real, this having to divide my things between them.

In any case, she's crying too hard to argue, and it's clear the couch and painting are the last things on her mind. Paul isn't here yet, so he has no idea of my interference on his behalf into his sister's projected machinations—which might not even exist. Maybe I just want to distract her.

Cringing, I begin to think about how to live what might be the last two to three years of my life while in the last stages of a disease I've never heard of. I take comfort in at least having notice.

Should I follow the acceptable protocols of putting my affairs in order? Retreat home in depression? Decide which of my possessions will go to whom? Who gets the Corosh painting? The Henredon down-filled couch? My jewelry? The antique wood Buddha sculpture from India? All the unusual, irreplaceable objects d'art collected in my travels? My Santa collection?

Just to be clear—I don't collect Santas. But my friends think I do because everywhere in the world I go, I come home with a new Santa. So, a few years ago, I began to get Santas as Christmas gifts. And of course, every Christmas season, I give them all a place to lounge in my home. But I'm not a collector.

Should I book myself into someplace in Oregon, where the Death with Dignity Act would allow me to take a lethal dose of a prescription drug given to me by a physician for me to self-administer? Under the Act, ending one's life in accordance with this law does not constitute suicide.

Two years from now, I'll be visiting a friend who's losing her vision due to macular degeneration. She's a visual, colorful, person with no desire to live in a world of darkness. The plan to have a doctor give her an injection of something that will put her to sleep permanently has been in place for some time. It's allowed in the country where she lives. Another friend will decide to give up her battle against a cancer that has metastasized through a large portion of her body and has a similar plan. I'll notice that many people of my generation have such a plan. We want to go on our own terms, not those dictated by laws or doctors okay with prolonging our lives by any means, no matter the pain it causes us.

Coming back to me. I could plan; arrange for my children and grandchild to be there with me. We could sit around and talk about philosophy, deep space, the awful foreign policies of this country sometimes, or about the fact we are certain aliens have come to Earth, about the state of our food supplies, about everything but the fact I'll be dead in fifteen minutes.

At some point, I'd fall asleep. Forever. They'd cry for a while, then get on with life because that's what their *maman* told them they should do.

No funeral. Instead, a huge, happy party. Anyone who wants to say something about me can, but is only allowed the mike for two minutes tops. Someone must stand next to the speaker with a stopwatch to ensure compliance. And what the speaker shares must be an anecdote about something they experienced with me, not just a story they heard about me.

Meanwhile, despite my forays into looking for treatments other than chemo or the other drugs on offer, the following refrains play over and over in my mind for the next two months, an awful discordant symphony.

"Should I do chemo after all?" "No, of course not." "Well, maybe." "What? No way!"

Such thoughts come in and out of my head, bees flitting to and fro looking for that just-right nectar.

"Well, what if nothing else works?" says Me. "What if I break more bones without it?" says Myself. "Chemo will kill you before the cancer does," say I. And on and on.

While, at this point, I still *know* chemo could kill me sooner, I begin to doubt in equal measures that the alternative stuff will work or will work for long. Plus—the money. Where will I get $60,000 to throw at a controversial treatment with no certainty? And that's just for two weeks of treatment. What about that third week they want me to stay? And what about afterward?

All this while I loll away my time in bed with little money coming in because I'm hardly working my business.

This, the year of my diagnosis, was to have led to my ultimate goal of supporting myself with writing only, something I projected would happen within two years. It started with that writer's conference in San Miguel de Allende, which I saw as the launchpad for my writing career. Plus, also booked; a three-week summer vacation to Canada to visit family and drive around aimlessly. In other words, a full, glorious year ahead.

Also in my near future, I saw a three-month trip to Southeast Asia to revisit Thailand, but also to go to the beaches of Vietnam, to Angkor Wat in Cambodia, and perhaps on to Bhutan from there. And another three months to the Greek Isles, Italy, to Barcelona and Ibiza where I haven't returned since spending many months more than thirty years ago. Not to forget a return to Amsterdam, the chaotic stomping grounds of my early twenties. How have things changed since I lived there?

Mostly, I want to see my daughter settle into her dreams, know her future children, see my son's daughter, currently my favorite granddaughter (she's my only), find her place in the world, my son reaching his dream of earning a living spending time doing the things where he feels challenged and where he makes a difference in the world instead of toiling away as a software engineer.

Really, I most want to finish as one who spent a majority of her time with books, reading them, and writing them with the hope to inspire and entertain others, traveling to places of interest and making friends there, and surrounded by the love of my family and close friends, in a home placed in the center of a grove of tall, majestic trees. Of course, it needs to be close enough to a town with great restaurants and live music venues. And water. A lake, the ocean, even a stream will do.

To me, that's goin' in style.

None of those things have happened yet. How can I leave?

In time, I'll see that a choice must be made. Take the route of living depressed and resentful for about three years and leave before ready.

Or this second route. I can get off the woe-is-me train at the next station and grab the feel-grateful-for-the-gifts-life-has-given-me connection. There are so many gifts! My two beautiful children whose presence in my life brings me the most joy and has taught me the best lessons; the work I've done that has helped many at a bad time in their lives; the glorious places on our blue planet I've been able to visit; the forays into metaphysics that take me on journeys to the ultimate frontier found deep in our minds; and love—finding love in the most unexpected things and places.

I choose the latter.

Close your eyes and take yourself through a day when you're angry, depressed, and resentful. Paint it black-hole black. See everything you'll do during such a day. Did you spill coffee in your car and can't find anything with which to mop it up? Did you catch every red light on your way to work? Did the principal at your child's school call for you to come pick them up because they're sick, or they participated in a prank on a schoolmate? Had a fight with your significant other? Burned the toast? Someone rear-ended you for no good reason? What else? Spend a few minutes with it, long enough to bring up the feelings such a day would give rise to; soak in them for a few minutes. How do you feel?

Now, run that same reel but make it a day on which you *choose* to feel happy, at peace, no matter the circumstance. A day where you realize that catching those red lights was a good thing as you drive by an accident two blocks beyond it. Might have been you, had you happened by even just a minute earlier. During that fight with your significant other a lot of air got cleared and you both feel happier as a result. Also, you decide to accept the thing that devastated your life.

You have cancer and might not live until this time next year? Find joy in the fact that *you got notice.*

You're blessed with the luxury to forgive those who need forgiving, to bury the hatchets of any ongoing squabbles, to tell someone you love them, to cry about sad things to purge them, to be present in the moment when around your family, to really absorb the love. You get to feel happy about the fact that the crape myrtle on your property will have bloomed when it's your time to go and you'll enjoy one last show.

There's always at least a glimmer of good in most bad. You just gotta dig for it as if digging for gold, bring it to light, allow it to shine.

And is knowing ahead of time you'll soon be gone from this earth, that you have the opportunity to do all of the above, not the glicken—the gold—in a devastating diagnosis? Imagine the alternative of having a fatal heart attack, or dying in a car crash, plane crash, or train crash instead. Look what you'd miss out on, the things you wouldn't ever be able to resolve.

I believe all that, yet, choosing the route of gratefulness and embracing the time I have left just doesn't feel like enough.

There's a desire for introspection. For asking myself, what does Maryse want? Rather than, what does the world want Maryse to want?

Sure, having notice is a good way to go.

Except I realize I don't want to go. Not yet.

Something shakes me out of this limbo, this purgatory into which I've buried myself. It nudges me to do all in my power to stretch time for as long as it will allow.

To see about getting done the things I wish I'd set out to do sooner in life.

In Limbo

My exit from the hospital and re-entry into the world occur in a haze with an underlayer of panic. A nurse does her best to prepare me by taking me there in steps. First, she wheels me to just outside the rehab hospital doors for a minute or two, a highly disorienting experience. I shrivel away from it. The next day, we stay outside a little longer, and she wheels me along a walkway lined with shrubbery, some flowering, others such a bright green, it hurts my eyes. The following day, we go a little farther along the path and I'm able to look at the shrubbery, flowers, and trees without cowering. Yet, it still feels as if I've entered a different dimension.

About an hour ahead of schedule, but not a minute too soon, my son, Paul, arrives to take me home. I should be mentally ready by now. But, much like the boy in the book and movie *The Room*, who at age eight was exposed to the outside world for the first time in his life, I feel overcome by the feel of the air around me, the sound of traffic, the smell of car exhaust, car horns, the difference in the sound of shoes when on concrete compared to pavement, people's voices outdoors, which sound different from inside, as if stretched thin, their voices having more air around into which to dissipate. These sounds had all been relegated to the back rooms of my mind from not having heard them in what seems like forever. Reintroducing them into my orbit feels like an exploration into a new world.

The unaccustomed motions involved in getting out of a wheelchair and into my car—an endeavor that takes a solid five minutes—slow me way down. It feels as though I'm part of a prison escape out of a film noir. As if my constricted ability will get me caught. As if someone might notice they weren't supposed to let me go (even though all the paperwork is signed, and two nurses spent a considerable amount of time helping me from a hospital gown to my own clothes and into a wheelchair).

What if allowing me to leave turns out to be a mistake?

I just want to get into my own bed. Once there, the next step might come to me, but right now, it's the end goal.

Dealing with serious post-traumatic stress, car rides still scare me—what with my back clenching and spasming at each small bump in the road, and memories of the agony of three ambulance rides fresh in my mind.

The ride to the house my children moved me into during my *incarceration* feels surprisingly smooth. Only four times does my back clench during the twenty-four-mile ride, my mind rocketing to panic. I am forced to take deep breaths, slowly in, slowly out, focusing on an image of waves breaking onto a beach and then ebbing, my go-to place during spasms.

It seems as if the spasms, the pain, the restricted movements, will forever remain a part of my life. I can't yet comprehend a time when enough healing will have occurred for me to do without a wheelchair, without a walker, without a full back brace.

As Paul pulls into the garage, a new challenge moves to the front of my mind.

This house was put into escrow eight days before The Event. When I was admitted to the hospital, two days remained to cancel escrow within our rights to do so. Yet Paul insisted that we continue with the purchase; he and my daughter would move me out of the condo and into the house. "We'll handle it, Mom. You don't need to do anything. You'll go home to your nice new house." Escrow closed three weeks before my release from the hospital, and as promised, all my things have been moved.

My new abode consists of two stories, living space downstairs, and three bedrooms, including a master suite with its own sitting room and Versailles-worthy bathroom. Mine. This morning, the idea is to get me into bed in that suite. That means me somehow overcoming an impossible challenge much like healing from a broken back and overcoming an incurable cancer: the staircase.

The thought of it brings back memories of the stairway at my condo, though this staircase is so wide it makes it impossible to use both banisters to help myself up. There is a landing halfway up and we discuss placing a chair there to give me a place to rest at the halfway point. But we discard the idea as it would most likely get in my way and presents a danger of tripping on it. Plus, sitting down and getting up takes a long time, and causes too much pain to warrant doing it halfway up or down.

I wonder how I'll get up and down the stairs to access the kitchen, for one, but with helpers at the house several hours each day, it turns out that I'll manage to avoid going downstairs for the next month. Head in the sand about it; same place it's at when it comes time to make a decision about cancer treatment.

If I don't think about it, it's not real. Right? Can't avoid thinking about my back because it comes with built-in alarms of pain and spasms, but multiple myeloma cells cruising through my bone marrow? I don't feel them every minute like my back. There's a name for keeping something like that in a locked room in my mind all by itself. Compartmentalization.

What if I can never again manage a staircase? Certainly can't use a walker while going up or down, yet I can't get around without one. In the end, one is left upstairs, the other downstairs, and while on the staircase I make heavy use of one side of the banister.

What had been a beautiful staircase to me when visiting and choosing that house now looks, and feels, like an insurmountable obstacle. I once wanted to climb Everest, and in my befuddled opioid state I think that might be easier to accomplish than ascending these stairs. Mental images of falling during a climb or descent, and breaking more bones, plague me.

"Come on, Mom, you can do it. I'm right here behind you," says the guilty one who talked me into continuing with this foolhardy move of, pun intended, moving me into a two-story house in my current condition.

"Yeah, easy for you to say," I grumble.

The house feels strange; I had only seen it twice during the purchasing process, and not since. Getting from the garage to the aforementioned staircase means walking down a hallway, and through the open-concept living room and kitchen. Seeing my furniture in that strange house makes the fact I now live here real, but in a surreal way.

Despite my fears, I think of how nice it will be to convalesce in the beautiful master bedroom—in my own bed. How nice it will be to spend time in the sitting room, to use the bathroom with its custom, high-quality tilework and wallpaper, high-quality granite countertop and sinks, shower and separate deep, deep, soaking bathtub. Nothing represents peace to me more than a soak in a bubble-fragrant bath, water up to my neck and the overflow drain jammed up with a face cloth to keep the water from escaping. Enough floor space left over for a good-sized club chair, though I'll never get to that because, at this time, unbeknownst to me, eighteen months later, the house will be sold, and I'll be moving 1,200 miles east to a new life near my son and granddaughter.

On that first day, though, reaching the second story and all the pleasures awaiting me there feels unattainable. Unattainable. As if the yin of living in that beautiful suite of rooms after close to ten weeks in three hospitals, and the yang of having to climb the stairs to get there, will never become a whole.

Yet, I can't help but fantasize, seeing myself in that tub, under a cloud of bubbles perfumed with lavender, sage, rosemary, and frankincense: scent, any pleasant scent will do. I covet getting my shattered self into that tub, a feat that will take three months to achieve with help, and another two months without, and which requires padding the tub with towels and a back cushion.

Right now, though, I'm still contemplating the staircase from the bottom of it, hanging onto a walker like onto a balcony rail and ensconced in that back brace.

Up I go.

One step at a time, both feet on each step before moving one up onto the next, pulling myself up with both hands on one handrail. I rest on each step, catch my breath, see myself on the next step before moving on to it. Tears of gratitude come to my eyes for having been given the strength to do it.

About five minutes later, I'm at the top, body shaking, sweat on my brow, a feeling of triumph coursing through me. Six months from now, it will take me about ten seconds tops to get up here.

Paul cheers from behind me all the way up. "Yeah, go, Mom! You're doing great!"

I roll my eyes and wish he'd shut up. Halfway up, I burst out laughing at the image of the two of us, me struggling in a back brace, hair with three-inch long roots and in dire need of a haircut, a grimace on my face at every step, Paul behind me yelling up encouragements like some crazed Cowboys cheerleader, or a Marine drill sergeant, the situation too ridiculous to do anything but laugh.

At the top, I barely pause, instead turning right to go into my bedroom—my bed, though I can't see it from this angle, so enticing.

Somehow, I manage to get into bed, but getting back out of it will prove to be a whole other challenge. The *give* of the mattress causes me to sink too low into it for my back to easily get itself back out of it. I need the harder mattress of a hospital bed. The bed arrives the next day with an uncomfortable mattress I endure rather than painful entries and exits from my usually most-comfortable bed. Plus, the fact I can raise and lower the back, as well as the height, helps greatly in getting in and out of it. Months later, I'll end up buying an adjustable bed base for my own bed.

On that first day home, it becomes clear that going up and down those stairs is out for some time to come. My children add a microwave and small refrigerator to my sitting room, though the microwave will remain for the most part unused, due to my lack of appetite and feeling averse to eating microwaved foods.

Lucky for me, a good friend for whom I'm ever thankful comes every day for two weeks when my children can't be here.

She cooks for me, helps me shower, changes the sheets, helps me into clean clothes, keeps my spirits up. Then follows a series of professional helpers who come for several hours every day to take over from my friend, who, after all, has a husband and son to look after.

Once home, though, my most immediate goal reached, I enter a mental space in which cancer doesn't exist, physical therapy doesn't exist, having to strap into that full back brace each time I leave the bed, using a walker to get to the bathroom, having to bring in a hospital bed... all of it gets relegated to a part of my brain on which I close the door.

It will be six weeks before I emerge from that space, forced to do so by my children, my sister, my few remaining friends, all clamoring for me to call an oncologist and a physical therapist.

It will be four months before I can manage things such as taking a shower without help, using a blow dryer, and making it down the dreaded stairs on my own, something I'm forced to start doing in order to go to physical therapy to get my body moving as it should. Again, yin and yang. Therapy is necessary and to get to it, it's necessary to conquer the behemoth of that staircase.

I resent being forced out of limbo. Luckily, some part of me knows that if I'm to remain here, here being in this life, an effort is called for.

The band-aid *must* be ripped off.

Across the Divide

The concept of yin and yang holds many facets, and various cultures see it in different ways. In Taoist metaphysics, it is seen as an indivisible whole—one can't do without the other. Among other things, Confucianism sees it as opposites, but strives to find the middle ground between the two to achieve balance in all things.

So, they're opposite, sure, but also comprise two sides that create a dynamic whole. Its very existence depends on both sides intermingling.

Opioids, which I take for five months after leaving the hospital, slow my progress once I decide to continue researching cancer treatments. They fog up my brain, which makes for foggy thinking and muddy decision-making.

Since at this point, I'm researching only what we call *alternative* treatments in this country, my internet research focuses on the realms of nutrition, supplements, treatments such as hyperbaric chambers, acupuncture, Chinese herbs, and the benefits of THCa, THC, and CBD. Many others will come across my radar later.

So far, I've conducted few searches on mainstream treatments because I fear what I think I know about all those chemo treatments, proteasome inhibitors, and immunotherapy. At this point, in my view, those will kill me faster, rather than save me.

Plus, I still believe less invasive, and less damaging alternative treatments will heal me for good, so I spend most of my waking hours doing online research.

No alternative treatment too woo-woo to consider.

No radical guru too out there to listen to.

Yet, at some point, thoughts of chemo begin to float about in the periphery of my consciousness, flotsam alternatively hitting the shore of my mind and moving away from it. Swooshing in, swooshing out...

Discouraged and frustrated by all the contradicting information, I once again drop the research, and let what I've found so far buzz about in my head like a swarm of bees, while asking, over and over, what the right thing is for ME.

I've landed in the only place I can think of for my answer.

Within.

You'd think it would have been the first place I'd go—it is me we're talking about after all—but I hesitate to trust myself to make the right choice. Didn't The Event occur due to a series of bad decisions made by me?

But, ultimately, the place where all answers reside *is* within. That is where doubt and hints that fuckery was afoot took place. Even my drug-addled brain knows it.

Slowly, my mind, faced with an earlier-than-wanted death, starts to consider chemo or similar treatments when it becomes clear that the money for treatment by alternative or holistic means only isn't materializing. And that, in any case, because the disease is so advanced, the alternatives aren't likely to do the trick on their own. They didn't help Steve Jobs despite all the money he spent on them.

Two months pass, months of emotional agony, of total mindfuck going back and forth. In the end, the dangerous levels of the disease in my body force my decision.

Before The Event, I hadn't seen an allopathic doctor in more than twenty years. I believed, based on propaganda from the alternative side, that they couldn't be trusted, that their game was to treat people with prescription drugs only, which did not heal them, but solely controlled symptoms.

So, making the decision to go with allopathic meds is a most difficult one, and completely out of the norm for me. Shame and regret spice up the soup of my emotions. Shame that I haven't found a better answer. And regret that I haven't found a better answer.

Yet, is dying really preferable?

I arrive at a reluctant decision. Still unable to leave my bed without the back brace that covers my whole torso (which makes taking a pee in the middle of the night quite an exercise in patience for my bladder), still on opioids and muscle relaxers, I make an appointment with an oncologist, "just to see."

The oncologist and his staff do all they can to reassure me. Despite my ramblings over my dread of chemo, they present me with the best-case scenario, assure me that I'm in good enough shape to see good results, all without making promises they can't keep. And without ever saying I'll survive...or that I'll soon die. After all, no one can know how my body will react to the drugs. Some people respond to it. Others don't. Just like any alternative treatment.

And no one loses their shit when I talk about acupuncture, high-dose curcumin, berberine, DHA, Vitamin D, and other possible cures.

I feel defeated. Like a samurai who's lost her honor. By agreeing to chemo, I dishonor myself by going against my principles. For a day or so, I consider seppuku (dying at my own hand), what a samurai does when he or she has lost their honor, has not been true to their own principles. Though, since disembowelment—the traditional way to commit seppuku—is beyond my tolerance, I'd most likely choose the pill route to end things.

After days of mental turmoil, I opt to swing both ways, a combo of what will turn out to be a proteasome inhibitor and alternatives. Later, I'll add a third element to the mix.

Reluctantly, I conclude that it's time for the yin to yang and the yang to yin.

Time for them to shake hands.

I can't force that on the world at large but can do it in my own world.

As an aside, for a lesson in humility, nothing works better than standing at the door to an infusion room the first time, looking at dozens of people hooked up to a drip knowing that a literal poison is being delivered into their bodies. The sight of that and the energy of the deathly illness that is cancer hits me like a cannonball. It stops me short in that doorway, nearly makes me turn around.

Can I really go in there and allow that stuff to be infused into my veins?

Can I not allow it and die instead?

No Getting High

The wall across from my bed approaches me, then recedes. It also changes from its usual whiteness to muted rainbow colors that undulate on it from left to right, from up to down, and back again. It's like watching the pixelation in a moving picture.

The THCa Justin provided me has failed. Again. THCa is not THC; you don't get high on it. The point of taking it is that it helps control nausea brought on by chemotherapy.

Ten years prior, a doctor in California became so enamored of the healing effects of cannabinoids on all sorts of ailments, as well as its ability to control side effects of chemo and similar drugs, that, the moment it became legal, he changed his entire practice to devote his time to prescribing them to patients. Fast forward a few years and this doctor would die from having tried to heal his own cancer strictly with THC. Sigh.

After a three-hour phone consultation with him, he prescribed a combination of THCa, CBD, and a small amount of THC to me. Two years later, I'll discover that, due to new studies, a combination of THC and CBD helps multiple myeloma patients best, and even better if used in tandem with carfilzomib, exactly the drug prescribed to me. Together, these cannabinoids cause the death of multiple myeloma cells (apoptosis), keep the live cells from moving around, and help control side effects of chemo.[1]

But on this morning, too stoned for my liking, I don't know this yet, so I still want to persevere with THCa.

Because I'm not fond of feeling high, I take THC at night only, and benefit from the side effect of it causing me to sleep deeply. For the first time in more than twenty years, sleep takes me away for at least seven hours a night, sometimes longer. This didn't even happen with the opioids.

Yet, studies on the effects of THC on sleep show that, in the short term, one sleeps better, deeper, feels more refreshed in the morning. In the long term this reverses. Study participants experienced broken sleep, not feeling as well rested, and experienced memory issues the next day. It also lessens REM sleep, reduces dreaming (no dreams at all when I take it at night), reduces the processing of emotions that usually takes place during REM, and keeps new memories from sticking. Somehow, I

---

1. https://www.ncbi.nlm.nih.gov/pmc/articles/PMC5363603/ https://www.mymyelomateam.com/treatments/medical-marijuana

must train myself to take it during the day, gradually increasing the dose so that I don't feel the high.

On treatment days, I still take it at night because it helps me get at least three to four hours of sleep since I'm infused with steroids along with carfilzomib—the conventional side of the fence's protocol for dealing with the side effects.

Later, I will fight against this, win, and end up taking less than a quarter of the universally prescribed dosage. With the cannabinoids in my system, that's all I need. This is a good thing, since I find the craziness—physical and mental—of the steroids' side effects difficult to handle. Imagine your body is exhausted, but your mind is so on fire that it directs your body to constant action. Want your kitchen cleaned well including cleaning out the fridge, and emptying the cabinets, wiping them down and refilling them at 4:00 a.m.? Take a dose of dexamethasone, the steroid in question.

The effects of various cannabinoids on side effects of chemo have been well researched.[2]

It further helps treat neuropathic pain (caused by damaged nerves), a side effect of the particular drugs prescribed to me. It must work as I've rarely experienced it.

As a side note, there's a faction of people who claim that large amounts of THC oil can cure any cancer after ingesting it for a few months. During my research on this, I'm referred to a friend who knows a woman who did so, and claims it cured her own

---

2. https://www.ncbi.nlm.nih.gov/pmc/articles/PMC5852356/

form of blood cancer. But my skepticism meter is vibrating in the red zone.

I'm all for anecdotal evidence, but where large amounts of THC for healing cancer are concerned, the "evidence" has been mostly gathered by people selling the stuff. The "proof" is from people hyping their own cure online, and the feeling of them looking for some glory overshadows their claims for me.

I'm not putting my life in their hands, especially since it means being very high all day and night for at least three months, the length of time proponents claim it takes to completely heal.

Before taking on a cure, I want to see (double-blind studies or wide anecdotal) evidence gathered by professionals, like medical researchers, MD oncologists, naturopath oncologists, and homeopaths who specialize in cancer.

I'd rather take my chances with the combination of chemo and CBD/THC, which has been researched.[3] A bonus for me is that the combo of CBD/THC does a great job of controlling side effects of the chemo for me—it doesn't work for everyone. I feel next to none, except fatigue.

Despite their many benefits, none of the studies say that THC and CBD, separately or together, cure cancer.

Also, CBD/THC isn't good for all cancers. In the case of some, new studies show that it even encourages the growth of tumors, so it's not something to take on blindly without

---

3. https://www.ncbi.nlm.nih.gov/pmc/articles/PMC5363603/

researching its effect on the specific cancer one wants to heal from![4]

The only snafu occurs when I want to also use THCa because at this point, I still believe it plays a role along with the others. Unless the side effects of a batch of THCa gone rogue turn out to make the walls undulate and my anxiety rise, which means it somehow converted to THC, and the high hits me unexpectedly.

Marijuana gets its high aspect when the leaves of the plant are artificially dried as in a low-temperature oven. Except for some reason, the leaves that Justin gave me appear "wet," the term used to say that the leaves have not been dried, not been converted to THC.

After I come down from feeling high a bit, I text Justin, who prides himself on his knowledge of all things cannabis, who grows his own, and who makes his own oils. Though he doesn't make a practice of keeping THCa around, usually converting all of it, he committed to supplying me with some. It can be difficult to find, because most end users are mainly interested in getting high or, if interested in healing, either don't mind the high or seek it along with the cure.

My phone rings within seconds of clicking Send.

"It's not possible," he says.

---

4. https://health.ucsd.edu/news/releases/Pages/2020-01-13-how-marijuana-accelerates-growth-of-hpv-related-head-and-neck-cancer-identified.aspx

"Well, I don't know what to tell you. The walls are still moving; I know that much."

He sighs in frustration.

"Where did you keep it? I mean, it must have been close to some sort of heat source." Me.

"I keep it separate from everything else for you."

"Did you grow this batch or get it from someone else?"

He sometimes obtains raw plant material from others if he needs more than his own small crop can deliver.

"I got it from one of my guys in Cali. I trust him..." But his voice wavers as he says it.

"Justin, this can't happen. What if I'd been driving?"

We end the conversation, but that's exactly what happens to me as, two weeks from then, I drive back home from having had lunch with friends. About five minutes from my house, the red traffic light at which I'm stopped starts to sway, but there's no wind. At all. I watch, mesmerized. Almost immediately, I get *the* feeling—you know, the one where you know in your body that your mind is high.

I grip the steering wheel, feeling nauseated—from fear, not from anything I ate. The realization that I'm way too high to be operating a motor vehicle hits me as if I've slammed into a wall.

It's just my brain doing that, it's not real, I tell myself as I watch the traffic light move back and forth like a porch swing moving sideways. What if a cop stops me? Paranoid, I try to remember the last time I checked if all my taillights lit up properly. At this point, I can pull over and wait for hours for the feeling to go away or continue home as carefully as possible. While still debating the question with myself, I make it home, five minutes away on quiet roads, gratefully pull into the garage, and skip kissing the ground; it's dirty, for one, and what would any neighbor happening by think?

As much as THCa might help, I can't trust Justin as a source anymore, or rather, I can't trust that his sources will deliver true THCa. And since accessing consistent batches of it proves difficult unless I grow it myself, the only thing to do is give up.

Meanwhile, I wonder if taking these cannabinoids along with mushroom powders, going back and forth on high-dose curcumin, will keep me well, keep me alive.

An undercurrent of doubt serves as a base from which all I do to heal springs. Something's still missing. Since I can't figure out what that might be, what else can be done besides push it to the side and pretend it's not there?

Can You See It?

In the wintertime in Canada, as a child trudging to school in slush and snow, I'd tell myself that once I reached adulthood, there would be no snow where I live. No snow to get into my boots and mittens or down my back collar as I stick my chin down into my coat for some warmth.

I thought of palm trees, imagined warm sun on my skin, envisioned dry pavement even in winter. Just like on television. I thought of it often with longing and could see myself in that environment.

At age fourteen, I ended up living in California for a summer, then Hawaii from age twenty-five to age twenty-nine, then on to Las Vegas, where I lived for a few decades. All warm places with no slush and snow in winter.

Caught in a bad situation at age seventeen where I needed a safe place to sleep, I sat in a coffee shop nursing a cup of coffee, imagining someone showing up, angel like, and saving me. My feelings about it overwhelmed me. I saw and expected an angel to appear each time the bell above the door clanged and someone walked in. Within two hours, my angel, a complete stranger to me, showed up and saved me from a night out in a cold wind.

At a time when I was single, I imagined meeting the perfect man for me, the type of man he was, how he'd treat me, and thought about it daily for several days—seeing myself walking arm-in-arm with him—at the end of which I met a man, who, at the time, turned out to be The One.

In each instance, I experienced naturally occurring good feelings brought on by positive thoughts about my wish. My feelings on the night I nearly spent outside leaned more to desperation than love, but my thoughts were about someone showing up to save me. And each time the door to that coffee shop opened, my heart lifted, anticipating my angel, and seeing myself being saved.

Feelings attached to all those strong thoughts brought the events to me, but at the time, I didn't realize what I was doing, didn't know that feelings attached to thoughts fueled them into reality.

Years passed, me sometimes getting what I visualized, and sometimes not, good and bad, never for a moment thinking that these thoughts, these feelings, brought on the actual events in my life. If anything at all, I saw these occurrences as coincidences.

It would be years before I came to know how dangerous picturing negative events is for us, how destructive. And though good things happened like the events described here, many more negative thoughts made their home in my head. And these, of course, brought on feelings to match.

When it became a thing people started talking about, I realized that what I'd engaged in during the events I mention here was visualization. Visualization differs from imagination in that when we visualize something we think and feel as if it's already happened.

When we imagine, it's more like looking at that car, that house, that vacation and thinking, wouldn't it be nice, sighing, and moving on. We don't see ourselves as the owner of the thing of our desire. When we visualize, we "sit" in that car that we own, live in that house; we are on that vacation. In other words, we see ourselves as owning the object of our desire, see ourselves with the result we seek on a test, medical or otherwise.

Upon my discovery of visualization and what can be accomplished with it, I engaged in it, but not all that seriously, not with intent, not with frequency, not with true belief that what I visualized would come true.

In time, for reasons I no longer recall, I gave it up, most likely because some other shiny object caught my attention.

The possibilities behind visualization returned to me while in the hospital, as I struggled to sit, stand, and walk. Visualizing myself standing and sitting in the wheelchair, then taking action. It worked. But, again, I left it at that despite my success.

Then, in the space of twelve hours, about eighteen months after The Event, I come across imagination as a tool for making things happen in one's life in the form of a friend's Instagram post. It triggers faint memories of the above-mentioned events.

For the first time, I realize that those things happened because I visualized them, took action, acted as if they'd already happened. Excitement courses through me. What if...

The next morning, I boot up my cell phone and without any particular action on my part—you know how technology sometimes sends you somewhere you need to be or see without any action on your part (serendipity, or Google stalking me?)—something shows up on my Instagram feed.

I stare at a post by Elizabeth Gilbert, author of *Big Magic*, *Eat Pray Love*, and other books. Her post tells of how she used imagination to get over her grief for her deceased partner.

Zapped twice with powerful imagination messages in a short span, even my chemo-addled brain pays notice. I feel inspired—no, compelled—to take all this further and add visualization to my healing bag.

Visualization is imagination on steroids, I decide.

While thinking that, I recall that in *The Power of Belief*, Bruce Lipton says that our mind can make our bodies do anything if we believe it. But to believe it, we must first imagine it.

Dr. David R. Hamilton, who helped develop drugs for cardiovascular disease and cancer for a large pharmaceutical company, says that, because of some of experiences he had while working there, he concluded that belief shifts biology. When he made this discovery, he left Big Pharma to educate people in "how they can harness their mind and emotions to improve their mental and physical health."

What if, I ask myself, I take imagination one step further and visualize instead to make my psyche believe I am one hundred percent healthy? What if? And why not? I mean, what could be the worst-case scenario? Nothing will change, and I'll have had some fun. Like acting *as if* but adding *feeling as if* to it.

So, I jump on the Visualization train.

It'll fix everything for me, you see. Who needs chemo or THC and derivatives, and Chinese herbal medicine, and curcumin, and whatever else caught my eye lately?

There have been studies done regarding how visualization affects athletes, but when it comes to healing, few doctors have been on board. One of the first was O. Carl Simonton, considered to have pioneered the mind-body connection when it comes to cancer treatment. He began his work in the early '70s, and though his method is still scientifically unproven, many people have had success with it in that their quality of life has improved and they have lived longer than expected.[1]

It took years for other doctors to take on his ideas and expand on them, such as by adding spirituality into the mix. Among others, we have Dr. Harold G. Koenig, director of the Center for Spirituality, Theology and Health, and Dr. Andrew Weil, who

---

1. https://www.latimes.com/nation/la-me-carl-simonton3-2009jul03-story.html

in 1994 founded the Arizona Center for Integrative Medicine at the University of Arizona College of Medicine in Tucson, where he still serves as director.

Encouraged by this, every day I revert to happy thoughts over and over, seeing myself as the healthy, vibrant woman I want to be, back to hiking miles and miles, doing forward bends like a yogi with hands flat on the floor like I used to, instead of my fingertips hitting just below my shins.

For months, I go on like this, walking for miles and miles, going on camping trips, getting into a sleeping bag on the ground, standing in the kitchen for long periods of time, cooking or baking, doing hour-long yoga classes, sleeping on my back, and my blood test results all being in the normal range.

In other words, seeing and feeling myself as I wish to be again. Because all of this happens in my thoughts only.

In real life, I can stand for ten to fifteen minutes tops before my back grumbles in protest, but it's an improvement over not being able to stand at all. No lying on the ground in a sleeping bag, but I feel confident it will happen one day. And my forward bends aren't hands flat on the ground, but I'm doing them, again, a vast improvement.

A month in, overall, I feel happier, more upbeat. I become more flexible, start to believe I can beat this thing. But nothing much changes medical-wise. Labs don't improve; a bone marrow biopsy shows that twenty percent of my white blood cells are still myeloma cells, crowding out the good ones, no doubt planning an attack the likes of which would make Napoleon or Hitler proud.

I accept that this alone isn't going to do it on its own either. Maybe I don't believe enough. Maybe I'm fooling myself.

Yet, I feel an inkling, something there in the back of my brain taking its sweet time to get itself to the front. It's as if I'm missing the cinnamon in my apple pie recipe, or the lemon in my Earl Grey tea, but what? What is it? And where is it? Whatever it is, I need it now.

My mind struggles to figure it out. Life goes on, me an automaton going through motions programmed by whatever powers run the Universe.

I begin to wonder, *Can I really get myself out of this one?*

Chemo Brain

I'm sitting in the infusion room, talking to the nurse as she's inserting a needle into my arm that will deliver a chemo drug into my veins. Multiple myeloma cells beware! I'm sending little soldiers after you. They'll eat, vaporize, or otherwise destroy you!

"I feel like I'm forgetting so many things these days," I say to the nurse. "And sometimes, I have a hard time working out problems in my head, like making choices, or I don't know, stuff like that."

"Oh, don't worry about it, that's just chemo brain!" She laughs as she says it.

"Chemo brain?"

"Yes, it's a side effect of these treatments. Most patients have some level of it."

"And that's why I'm forgetting stuff? Or making wrong decisions?"

My heart flutters and hiccups.

"Yup. It goes away at some point."

"At what point?"

"Depends on the person. The average is about six months."

"Six months! You mean, six months after I no longer get treatments, or six months into the treatment?"

She stops what she's doing and looks me in the eye. "After treatment stops." She resumes her infusion room nurse thing with needles and tubing.

While I try to digest this, infusion pumps—about thirty-two in the room I'm in—beep on and off, letting nurses know when an infusion bag holding the poison, I mean, the medicine , has emptied out, signaling the patient is done for the day, or that it's time for their next infusion if they're getting multiple drugs that can't be simultaneously infused.

"Oh. I thought, you know, maybe the mind gets used to it?" I finally ask.

"Nope, unfortunately, it doesn't work that way. It'll be all right, don't worry."

Sure. That's what my ex-husband said just before he joined a religious cult.

It doesn't help that she laughs as if losing one's memory is no more important than losing a paper clip.

Despite their complications and side effects, chemo, proteasome inhibitors, monoclonal antibodies, and immunotherapy drugs helped saved my life, no doubt about it. I am grateful.

Still, how to deny their side effects on the brain (in addition to the damage done to the body)? How thoughts get jumbled the way a clothes dryer tangles clothes. Or how, standing at the bathroom sink still wearing that dammed back brace—because it's too risky to stand without it with the drug *du jour* weakening me—I brush my teeth. And then, do it again. Because my brain isn't signaling that I just did that.

Where'd you go, mind of mine?

One harrowing example is an incident that occurs about two years into getting treatments on the regular. By then, I function well. I've resumed life enough to work in a limited capacity, write, and travel, though carefully. And, no more back brace.

On a day when I feel stronger, I sign up for an online writing class on Character. As usual when it comes to writing classes, I can't wait to start. Week One goes well, and I save assignments in their own folder on my computer. It's when the teacher sends me his notes for Week Two of the course that things go way wonky. I've forgotten the name of the class folder, so I do a computer search to find it.

The search returns not one result, but two. Just below the folder named Character Class—what I've named the class's folder—there's one named Character. What the hey...

My blood pressure rises; my face flushes. Please say it isn't so.

What will I find when I open the Character folder? Eyes wide on it, I click on the small yellow folder icon. There, sitting innocently, holding a neutral position, are three subfolders: Week1, Week2, Week3.

WTF?

I open each subfolder and there find not only the assignments for the class but comments from the teacher. Which means I've not only taken the class *but participated in every lesson and even got feedback from the teacher.* In the end, it becomes clear that I took the class about six months before The Event based on the dates the folder and subfolders have last been accessed.

But I recall none of it.

This is "chemo brain" at its best. Or rather, its worst.

Sometimes the Universe Just Likes to Fuck With You

In 1994, at barely age forty, I scheduled a visit with the plastic surgeon who gave me breast implants eighteen months before. I'd asked for my breasts to be restored to how they looked before nursing two babies; a mommy makeover before it became mainstream.

Fast-forward a little more than a year post-surgery, when the urge to get those things out of me slams me relentlessly. I wake up thinking about it—and go to sleep thinking about it. Out with the Dolly Parton–sized tatas (the surgeon had given me larger implants than I'd wanted), says my every thought.

More than the size of them, though, I feel something's not right. No proof, no reason, just a feeling.

It takes me three months to pick up the phone and make the appointment.

I tell the surgeon about my feeling.

He finds a lump in my left breast.

Sends me for a mammogram that doesn't show the lump.

He orders an MRI, which shows it.

The next day comes a biopsy.

Three weeks later, I'm at work in the production office of Cirque du Soleil when I get The Call. Stage I of a rare cancer that usually mimics itself in the same spot on the other breast.

There are many tears, a trip to the library with a friend-colleague whose office I ran into after the phone call. There, we pick out a bunch of books on the subject. She also arranges a conversation with an ob-gyn friend who helps me understand the test results better.

In the end, I land at the Susan Love program at UCLA. Dr. Love, considered controversial by some because of her ideas to avoid aggressive surgery and chemo treatments, founded the National Breast Cancer Coalition, and wrote what is considered the "Bible" for women afflicted with breast cancer, *Dr. Susan Love's Breast Book*.

A month later, I find myself at the hospital on the campus of UCLA having the surgery. I then recuperate in LA at the house of a cousin who'd agreed to take care of me until my follow-up appointment and until doctors cleared me to go back home.

Once back in Las Vegas, I undergo twenty-five radiation treatments. I believe the cancer will never come back.

Except it does.

Twenty-four years later, eighteen months after the multiple myeloma diagnosis, bam.

I'm diagnosed with breast cancer. Again.

This should hit me hard, except—nothing. Some would refer to my attitude as cavalier, detached, disconnected.

They wouldn't be wrong, but there's more to it than that.

Not long before my new diagnosis, I began a daily practice of something called quantum meditation (where one goes into the subconscious with the intent to reprogram it to what one wants to make happen in the three-dimensional world). Thousands claim it either healed them or played a large part in their healing. I belong to the latter group.

All who tout it out there on the innerwebs approach it differently, have a different explanation and method for engaging in it. The commonality I found with many has to do with reaching out into the energy field around our bodies and beyond. You put out there what you want with your mind and attract it back with your heart.

In between meditations, you take it beyond that and behave and feel, and live your life as if what you want has already happened, as if it's going on right now.

Proponents have been exposed to it by among others Deepak Chopra, with his quantum healing philosophy, and in recent years by Joe Dispenza (who goes by Dr. Joe), as well as by some organizations, including one in India that has made it its mission to expose as many people worldwide to their version of it as possible.[1]

Each who touts it explains it in their own way. I've done at least one meditation offered by all the groups I found. Since I'm not a doctor or a scientist, the simplest explanation I can give is that it works from a place of restoring equilibrium to our energy centers, which presents an environment of wholeness for our cells and calms the mind.

I want to wholeheartedly believe it will heal me like it's done for others. At the very least, after reading an entire book on it, and multiple articles, I come to believe it will help restore balance to my body. It alleviates my stress and anxiety and makes me feel as if I have control over this thing that has invaded me right down to the marrow of my bones. It acts as a linchpin around all the healing protocols in my Heal Maryse Bag.

The naysayers say it's hogwash; these are the same people who look at everything new in medicine as charlatanism and see the Deepak Chopras and Joe Dispenzas and Bruce Liptons as quacks and pseudoscientists. No doubt it's their grandparents and great-grandparents who pooh-poohed Pasteur for daring to suggest germs cause disease, and who had something to do with the death of Dr. Semmelweis, who dared to claim, *and prove*, that handwashing helped save the lives of mothers and infants when practiced by doctors before assisting at births.

---

1. https://quantummeditationsociety.org/

Some say Joe Dispenza's definition of quantum mechanics isn't logical. That his claim that we can heal ourselves by tapping into our subconscious, going into what he calls "the field," or into the quantum, is *caca del toro* (my words). Others claim that if it works, it's just because of a placebo effect.

But, do I care if how he describes what he calls quantum meditation doesn't satisfy his critics? If it's not exactly in accordance with how quantum scientists would describe it, or precisely how they explain quantum mechanics? It works for me.

If you end up in Rome, does it matter what the road that got you there was named, or how it was described? You're sure to find at least one person who will try to convince you that the road you took is the wrong one. And yet, you're there.

We all have different feelings about different things. It's why Baskin-Robbins offers thirty-one flavors: not everyone likes the same one.

At this point in my journey, I want and need to believe in the likelihood of healing at one hundred percent. And there are now more and more studies that prove the benefits of the placebo effect if indeed it's what I'm getting out of it.[2]

In the end, I just care that it does the trick. At this point, no one can explain how or why it works.

---

2. https://www.ncbi.nlm.nih.gov/pmc/articles/PMC6013051/ https://www.health.harvard.edu/mental-health/the-power-of-the-placebo-effect

And I'm beginning to realize that it's not so much the Universe fucking with us, but the fact that, over our lifetime, our energy field has been collecting emotions thrown into it by virtue of the environment in which we live, and by our life experiences. It's simply returning to us what we sent out into the field.

The only way to keep the Universe from sending us what we don't want is to stop sending what we don't want into it.

When Death Takes a Pass

Multiple myeloma is rare, they say, except, of course, it doesn't seem that way to those of us who have it. The consensus is that it's incurable. Only a small percentage of those afflicted go into full complete remission (no sign of it in the results of a blood test). Even fewer reach stringent complete remission (no sign of it in blood test results and bone marrow biopsy), which equates to reaching the top of Mount Everest for the afflicted. And even after we've reached that lofty place, we're told, the cancer can come back at any time, that pesky relative you can't stand who keeps showing up at your door at dinnertime.

And some of those afflicted also suffer from many other issues brought on by it, infections because our white blood count is low, as well as liver and kidney issues and sometimes failure. Also, broken bones, although rarer nowadays—is a part of the deal of having a cancer that eats your bones. If diagnosed soon enough, there are drugs to keep them from breaking. But they come with a bag full of their own nasty side effects. Sometimes, it feels as if taking one drug just replaces the issue for which you are taking it with another that it brings on.

Despite all this, nine months into my diagnosis, I discover something surprising, something that lights up my soul.

Since The Event, my family and I believed, lived, and planned around the hospital doctor's prognosis that I'd die within three to five years. The more advanced the disease at the time of diagnosis, the shorter the remaining lifespan for the patient.

My initial research showed that an average patient at Stage III has a twenty-nine-month life expectancy. And I'd skipped to the front of the line at Stage III.5.

While in shock, my family and I hadn't immediately thought to dig deeper into the death sentence so cavalierly handed to me. Discouraged by our initial findings, and assuming that the doctor must know his stuff (no idea why we believed this, especially me, who, at the time, had little faith in allopathic doctors), we all only looked at the first few online search results—which concurred with him.

In other words, we drank the Kool-Aid without asking for the ingredient list first, something we all did, always, everywhere else in our lives.

Sharp emotional pain created by the surface information our online searches garnered kept us from looking at the thing too closely, the way many of us feel compelled to turn away from a dead body in the street, gore in movies, and bloody scenes in the news. We know it's there; we just don't want to see it. And to avoid feeling the unease that thoughts of it bring on, we also turn our minds away.

After those few cursory searches on prognosis, I slammed down my tablet cover, mentally blocking myself from conducting them. Why do something that causes such a deep level of emotional pain?

So, I turned my back on such searches until at least eight or so months after diagnosis—I saw no sense in dwelling on it.

Instead, I told myself *I* would heal, dammit. Forget what the proof facing me said. Just forget it.

But now?

"Paul, I heard something that means not everyone dies from this thing," I say to my son once I'm pretty sure my new information holds up after moving on to pages 2 and 3 of Google search results. Among other things, I discover that new drugs capable of extending the lives of multiple myeloma patients are headed our way at nearly the speed of light.

Still no cure, though.

Like someone afraid to name an evil so as to not attract it, I rarely say the name of my condition out loud.

"How?" he asks, so much caution in that one word. Much later, he'd tell me about his conversation with the pronouncement-of-impending death doctor soon after the doc had given me the news.

"What point is this at? He told me he'd asked the doctor. "Should we get her affairs in order?" The doctor responded that it would be very good idea.

"Dr. Sanchez says that he has a patient who had it like, twenty years ago, I think he said. And he did chemo and a stem cell transplant, and it's never come back. I don't know why he never told me this before. Well, I guess he had no way of knowing how my body would react to treatment."

Suddenly, we're both on pause. No doubt the same thing going through my mind goes through his. Only the usual background noises of a cell phone tell me he's still on the line. In a commercial, one of us would be asking, "Can you hear me now?"

We enter limbo.

The updating of my living trust, the assumption of my impending death, how I want my remains to be handled (my ashes buried in the ground and a tree planted in their center because I want to be a tree in my next life), what to do with my material belongings. Spending as much time together as possible. All that had been unnecessary, had been too soon?

"Mom? What do you mean that, you know, people don't have to die from it?" My daughter. She calls and says this in lieu of hello not even five minutes after my conversation with her brother. She, like me, always hesitates to call *it* by its name.

This latest bit of news confuses us, but propels us all to embark on new searches, going deeper into the prognosis for those afflicted.

I waver between frustration about it still being in my body and jubilation over the fact I might have time.

A chance.

A chance to achieve my life goals: writing full-time and earning a living from it, imparting what I know to others who ask for it, traveling to places far-flung from my home, seeing my children blossom in their own lives, having my young granddaughter, Olivia, beg me to take her for a manicure and pedicure, again, or to take her to a bookstore (where I'm in for it at the cash register!). I want to watch her run to me for a hug, listen to her talking about boy troubles when she's older. I want to watch her wave a diploma about and throw a flat board cap up in the air, and to be at her destination wedding.

Despite the better news, I so worry about the side effects of chemo drugs that I won't even look at the literature on them, won't discuss them, as if doing so will bring them to me. Still, I know they exist, and, five months into treatment I take a break from them even though my blood test results still show a decent amount of multiple myeloma cells. I know that both the disease and the chemo are wreaking havoc in my body, plus, there's chemo brain.

Though he says I should continue, there's no freak-out on the part of the oncologist over my decision. Plus, I crave beach time. I reason that my blood test results are flirting with normality because they look so much better than at diagnosis, so there's no reason not to go.

The doc agrees to give me a white blood count booster so I don't catch any cooties while on this trip I shouldn't go on.

At this point, being my optimistic self, I assume my body will continue what the chemo started and heal on its own, that I'll never have to do chemo again. Pfft.

I think that because there's a natural cure for my incurable cancer, based on information deep on a government health website. The article states that a woman in China who'd been diagnosed with multiple myeloma twenty years prior had been too sick to continue with chemo drugs. She'd chosen to visit her local acupuncturist instead. He'd prescribed a Chinese herbal remedy for her, and it had kept her in good enough health for all the years leading up to the time the article was written.

So, off I go in search of an Oriental medicine doctor to prescribe and obtain it for me.

Things look great.

No more chemo. *This* will save me.

My life will be normal again.

So, why not act as if all is well and go on a little trip?

Act as if all the pain, the suffering, the fatigue, the chemo-induced rashes on my hands, the looking at thick, long strands of my hair on the shower floor and clinging to my hairbrush like to Velcro, as if anything associated with my condition is behind me? Way behind me.

As if *the* cure has been handed to me. Because it has, I reason. So, why not?

Between the Chinese herbal remedy and various mushroom powders I also take, my ego leads me to believe that I'm all set.

I don't need any of that chemo stuff; I'm not going to fall for it again. Big Pharma is evil.

My spirits lift at the impending trip, true, but I worry about going alone despite having traveled the world on my own several times to places as far-flung as Singapore and Thailand.

Yet, a part of me knows there's no time for panic. So, I go all *Instagramy* on it, and Stick Fear into the Fuck It Bucket.

So, me and my magical Chinese herbal remedy take ourselves off. I don't dare travel with THC and CBD. The beach will also help with my healing. The energy at the point where saltwater meets beach sand has been proven to be the best place to get grounded and heal. All these things together, I reason, will cure me.

Is it part of our human makeup that we lie to ourselves when we really want something to be true?

There aren't any direct flights between Las Vegas and Puerto Plata in the Dominican Republic. For me, because of the time difference, getting there means spending the night at a hotel at Miami International Airport to then catch an early-afternoon connection the next day, which means retrieving my suitcase from baggage claim, lugging it to the hotel, and doing it all in reverse the next day.

But on this trip, things get even more complicated because the first leg of my flight is postponed until the next day. This means I need to retrieve my suitcase from baggage, go back home for the night, and return to the airport the next morning, checking in my suitcase again. And go through security. Again.

All this while wearing a large back brace because my back still sometimes gives out without warning, like a marionette flopping forward when the string holding its back breaks. I no longer wear it full-time, but having to lug a suitcase, to pull it off the carousel at baggage claim, and walking for miles and miles in the Las Vegas and Miami airports demands it because it means moving my body in all sorts of ways my physical therapist has advised against.

The problems with my trip to the beach reflect how I've been handling my healing journey. Fits and starts and breaking rules. Always breaking rules.

Once at the beach, each morning, at a much slower pace than on previous visits, and still wearing the danged back brace, impossible to hide under beach clothes, I stroll along the sand for about twenty minutes. Standing at the edge of the water, I breathe in the briny scent of the salt water, of the vegetation that the heat enhances. Bliss. With my sister, who lives there, I eat most evening meals at one beach restaurant or another. Nothing but beach, beach, beach for *moi*.

Throughout my life, I've been to many beaches in Holland; in Sitges and Ibiza in Spain; Vancouver Island; many beaches on Long Island, New York; on Oahu, Maui, Kauai, and the Big Island in Hawaii, most islands in Tahiti; in Thailand north and south, and at least a dozen Southern California beaches.

Nothing compares to the healing energy I've found on many of the beaches of the Dominican Republic. When you first step onto the sand, it feels like crossing through a portal, *Stargate* style. At least, some of the beaches there have that effect on me.

The beach, the Chinese herbal remedy, and the mushroom powders will heal me. I'm all set.

Three weeks later, I return home. Due for a checkup with the oncologist, I make the appointment, anxious to be told things haven't progressed, multiple myeloma–wise. Because, after all, I've been diligent about taking my magical herbal Chinese remedy.

The lab results from the blood draw during that visit send my mood spiraling down like an oil drill hitting nothing but rock. My whole body shakes, not to mention my mind.

I've been so certain that this was It, that I've found the cure, *my* cure. So much so that I feel offended it hasn't worked. Truly offended.

The labs show an unmistakable hike in the numbers that pertain to multiple myeloma. Too high to ignore.

The doctor says it could have been worse; that he's surprised they haven't climbed more.

So. My magical cure did something, but not enough. Just like the Dutch boy who plugged the dike with his finger. It wasn't enough to forever hold back the force of the water. And my magical Chinese herbal remedy isn't enough to push back against this dreaded disease on its own either.

I take myself back to the beach mentally, hanging on to anything that might enhance my mood because I know that bad feelings create bad energy, which eventually leads to chaos in my body.

I stop taking the Chinese remedy, not only because it didn't work well enough, but because the acupuncturist who prescribed it initially can no longer obtain it, and I can't find anyone else to get it for me. I continue taking the mushroom powders, adding them to my morning matcha tea, but begin to doubt their efficacy. I start my research from scratch. Strategize all over again. Sulk.

And start a new chemo regimen...

Lies Lies Lies

This time, the doc has me on just one injectable chemo drug, but only because the pill-form drug usually taken in combination with it doesn't agree with me. We'll see how it goes with just the one, he says. It involves a poke in the tummy twice a week. Quick to administer, but high on the pain scale. I also take a steroid to control side effects, which wires out my brain and keeps me from being able to relax despite exhaustion. This runs out my adrenals; another thing to deal with.

Meanwhile, I feel compelled to do everything that's important to me in life, except that, especially on chemo days, I'm ready to go to bed for the night by three o'clock in the afternoon, but it's a fallacy.

The steroids keep my mind too alert to sleep, except for about three hours for which I can thank the CBD and THC, which I've resumed taking after my return from the beach. I drag my exhausted body out of bed at around 4:00 a.m. because lying down has become boring and frustrating since sleep won't take me. Plus, my back, healed by quite a lot by now, displays a major quirk. I can do a lot with it now, except for one thing: lie on it. That, it protests with pain so deep I think something's breaking again. I sleep on my side but prefer to be on my back when it comes to thinking in bed.

And, I think. A lot. So, best get out of bed and sit in the recliner chair I've purchased for this purpose. This is when I began my middle of the night trysts with my kitchen cabinets, emptying them, wiping them down, then putting everything back. Oh, and I might as well clean the fridge while I'm at it. Sheesh.

I have to do more. Or less, in some cases. I tend to throw too much into any new project. And then, there's no way to know what worked when it does. Chinese herbal remedy, mushroom powders, cannabinoids, and—before I quit taking it because I thought it responsible for an awful rash on my hands—eight grams of curcumin every day.

With all these at once, how do I know which one helps with keeping multiple myeloma cells from growing as fast as expected?

I realize that my healing calls for more discipline and planning.

My mind munches on that.

I sense that more than just how I approach various remedies must be brought into the mix. How we think and how we feel affects outcomes in our lives, as well as our physical health. Even science knows this now.

Based on this, hard decisions face me. Healing requires more than changing my diet and taking a bunch of mushroom powders, magic herbal potions, THC, CBD, and THCa, and doing my best to focus on the positive.

Action is needed in other areas of my life too. Off with stress, for one. But how? The biggest stressor in my life is a small business that takes up too much time for too small of a financial result, but it constitutes the better part of my income. I long ago lost my passion for it but stayed out of concern over not being able to reproduce the income and lifestyle it brings me.

What if I lived the life I've dreamed of since forever, instead? Even if it only lasts a few short years?

Do I have the courage?

The courage to leave behind all the things in my current life that mean little to me? Things, habits, and people whose roles I've cut out of the movie script of my Ideal Life that plays in my head only?

We become so accustomed to the way our lives play out. Everyday habits, people we've known for years but don't particularly like, and even don't like at all sometimes, jobs we hate, partners we've outgrown. It's as if double-sided tape keeps us stuck to them. So, how can we separate ourselves from it all?

With my blood results headed in the wrong direction and the three to five years possibly still hanging over my head considering my latest lab results, there's little time for mulling it over: I must act NOW.

Out of these thoughts comes forth a deep desire to live creatively, to abandon conventions. It blooms in my mind like a lotus flower opening in the morning, but eventually never closing come nightfall. A plan seeps through. Soon, what to do next comes to me quickly.

After much mental turmoil, I distance myself from friendships that do nothing to enhance my well-being. Toxic friendships are ended abruptly.

Material possessions are given away. Lots of them.

Expectations are rerouted to more realistic outcomes for any remedies or healing protocols I embark upon. No more thinking I've stumbled upon a wonder cure each time I read or hear about some potion or other reported to be It. Becoming, and remaining, healthy necessitates more than throwing a bunch of supposed cures into my bag of tricks without any forethought. Each must be thoroughly researched and used on its own for a while to evaluate the results before keeping it permanently.

Executive decisions about my business that will lessen my stress and still provide me with a living from it are made. I'll think tomorrow about how to leave this completely behind too.

The biggest change occurs when I sell my home in Las Vegas and move to the Dallas area. I'll be near my son and granddaughter, and far away from toxic people, and others who, as kind as they might be, are already deciding between wearing gray or black to my funeral.

The move, like my healing journey, has a few rough patches, but in the end, I start a new life, one in which I've shed the baggage that dragged me down. It means hiccups in my treatment too, because a new chemo protocol must be started and it's a rough time.

This is repeated a year later because the first protocol I do in Dallas, a treatment that initially requires me to sit in a chemo chair for nearly three hours twice a week, one that sucks all the energy out of my body, siphoned from it like gas from a car, fails. The adjustment to this second protocol since I've moved proves worse than the first one.

Despite this going on, and my resolve to not throw alternative remedies at the thing like confetti at a wedding, never knowing where it will land, I continue to do so, choosing to look the other way as to how this might affect me, choosing to not dig into the reasons for this behavior of mine, which could well take me right to death's door.

It's easier to lie to myself. Well, for a while anyway.

I Decide

I turn over to see if I'll feel any better lying on my left side. Nope; maybe I feel somewhat worse. Fever steams out of my eyes, beads of sweat pearl at my forehead, nausea grips me. I bunch up my pillow to raise my head a little. Pull the duvet up around myself, and before it even lands around my shoulders, I'm kicking it off because I'm hot. Then, pull it back up almost immediately because I'm freezing.

I "toss" myself over back to my right side, a move that, in my head, takes three seconds. But in real life, it takes at least a full minute.

It's the headache, you see—the faster I move, the more it hurts. Moving slowly means it might not notice I've changed my center of gravity and punish me for it with earthquake eruptions sure to hit a 10 on the Richter scale.

And my stomach, so bloated it reminds me of being eighty percent of the way through my two pregnancies: Well, there's a demon dance going on in there now. And the demons are throwing spears at one another if the sharp pains constantly hitting my stomach's walls from the inside is any indication. And if I'm not mistaken, they're boiling a cauldron of something very fizzy. And it's getting bubblier by the second.

I can't take acetaminophen, or anything else, for my industrial-sized migraine. I already tried, and the demons sent it right back up. Antacids? Same result. They would allow no intrusion of any kind as they paced themselves through acrobatic contortions in my gut.

A couple of times, my bladder forces me up despite the cacophony in my head and mayhem in my belly. Standing causes me to nearly faint. Hands flat on the wall for support, dragging myself along it, I make it to the bathroom.

It's hard to see what you're doing when something is stabbing the inside of your head in staccato fashion, *zing zing zing*. After, I walk back to bed with eyes closed, my body bent nearly in half, my hands attempting to grip the wall this time, an impossibility. I feel tears on my cheeks without having first noticed that I'm crying.

The night passes like that. Hours, the next one just like the one before, me embedded in a cradle of pain the likes of which I haven't felt since I broke my back—almost *exactically* to the day, twenty-four months before.

I'm home alone. And during the time I might have still wanted to call for help, I found myself unable to reach for my phone; it was on another planet all the way over there on my night table.

But it doesn't matter. In the very early morning, I lose all desire to even want help.

I just want it to end.

I feel ready.

I say a little prayer for Death. To take me. Quickly.

She's in the room; I can feel her. She startles when she realizes this.

Silently, I beg. *Take me.* But despite prodding at my door so rudely, so loudly, so insistently, when I finally surrender, she hesitates, starts to retreat.

Please. *Please.* I beg, still feeling her, right *there*, cloaked Romulan style.

No response.

By early afternoon, my mind begins to find its way out of the ravages of my body, surprising me by its presence. *I have a brain* seems to be its first observation. And it apparently has its own cleansing, its own reckoning, in mind, no pun intended. Also, my emotion wheelhouse does its own flips, walks its own tightrope.

What will I do since it doesn't appear I'll die today after all?

Death seems to have left the building; the energy around me feels...lighter, different.

Mentally, I go over all the medical protocols and all the alternative things I've tried in order to heal. They're jumbled in my brain like cheap clothing in floor bins at a bargain basement T-shirt shop.

Tried. That word stands out the most. I've *tried* treatments.

I think about that for a minute. That's it...

I've been trying, not doing, says my muddled mind.

Yoda's face appears to me as he says, "Do. Or do not. There is no try."

Something prompts me to take it one step further and add: There is no half-ass doing either. Doing things half-assed is essentially just trying. I've been *half-assing* my way through healing protocols. That's the wrong way to engage with anything of importance, like healing. I'm all for going with the flow, but without a North to aim my flow at, to keep redirecting myself to, it's not possible to ever reach the place, the result, I seek.

There's no conviction behind try. And if we're like my mother, which I appear to be at least in this way, consciously or unconsciously, our attempts will amount to failure. In my case, until now, trying has been a product of my unconscious, embedded there by repeated early exposure to my mother's behavior in this regard.

What if I actually *do* instead of try?

This scares me because who knew that's what I'd been doing? It elates me. Thrills me. And scares me again. But isn't a goal worth pursuing always a little scary?

Doing this requires a complete mindset change on my part. My heart thumps against my rib cage. Did I not work on changing my personality? Just tried it, apparently.

To be fair to myself, I felt a sense that I needed a plan, but that the clock on the hours left in my life ticked loud and fast. The compulsion to try everything at once, right now, or else I'd die, influenced everything.

I sit—or rather, lie—with that realization for a few minutes. It seems I should feel disheartened—all that wasted effort and time—but, instead, hope begins to seep through my shroud of pain.

For reasons unknown, my mind presents me with an image from my childhood, my mother at our front door buying one gadget or another from a door-to-door salesman. Her purchase surprised me because my mother suspected everyone and anyone of being out to get something out of her, of trying to rip her off.

A new stain remover guaranteed to take that grass out of her children's clothes? "Pfft, it's a 'come on,'" just meant to make her buy the stuff. *And yet she'd buy some.* And then use too little of it and not let it soak in the garment long enough, ensuring failure.

My father showed her their bank account at about the time they retired from their respective jobs and said they could afford to go on a nice trip once a year. "Pfft, we'll see. I don't believe him," she said to me. She ignored the proof in the bank account and the multiple trips they went on. And so on with everything presented to her all her life, at least the part of it when I knew her.

Once, in my late forties, I visited her and my father. She couldn't wait to tell me that she'd just bought a curling iron she'd seen on an infomercial, saying proudly, "They sell it on

TV," as if TV was the final authority on everything good and trustworthy. *When did she decide this?* Yet, she followed that pronouncement with: "But, it probably won't work. Oh, well. I'll try it."

She went through the motions *while not believing that what she bought would work*. She was *trying* things, *never believing they'd work*!

I could ponder why that was, and why I've been doing it too, but there's something more important to address.

I open my eyes and fixate on the Buddha that sits in the center of my dresser right across from my bed. My mother must have handed down that quirk of hers to me by osmosis. My eyes fly open as I realize it's how I've dealt with many things in my life, including everything added, then discarded, from my healing regimen.

I "bought" them *without believing they'd work*.

My heart thuds harder against my chest wall. A thorough mental examination of all the things I've tried to heal myself follows.

I catch my breath. I thought *all the things I tried*, instead of *all the things I've done*.

Because.

It's proof that I *have* been only *trying*. With everything. That truth looks as vibrant to me as the morning sun in my eyes when I lift the window shades at sunrise.

A parade of all the healing protocols I've tried makes its way through my thoughts, crazed floats going down the street at Mardi Gras, some colliding with others.

I've *tried* chemo, reluctantly, and never questioned frequency and dosage. Instead, I pretended to myself I wasn't doing it. And it's been shown that the emotional state of cancer patients undergoing treatment can affect its efficacy.[1]

How had my attitude, my feelings, affected treatment?

That said, no matter what, considering my reaction to it, it's clear I'm getting too much with this new protocol started eight weeks ago when the previous one failed.

Not being the average when it comes to dosage of anything, I should have realized this and done something sooner. Acetaminophen makes me high. Antibiotics and antihistamines knock me out like a sleeping pill. Those opioids and muscle relaxers I took for six months after breaking my back? I lived those months ensconced in an alternate reality bubble, its edge fuzzy like cotton balls.

Does it not follow reason that my body needs less than the average person when it comes to chemo, too?

Note to myself that if I'm to continue it, this must change.

I've *tried* this diet, that diet, following the latest one purported to be the magic bullet for controlling multiple myeloma.

I *tried* various supplements and dosages.

---

1. https://www.takingcharge.csh.umn.edu/how-do-thoughts-and-emotions-affect-health https://www.healthline.com/health-news/can-positive-attitude-help-defeat-cancer#Can-positivity-cure-cancer ?

I *tried* THC and CBD and THCa.

I *tried* quantum meditation. Without the true belief and faith needed for it to work.

I *tried* that Chinese herbal remedy.

I *tried* medicinal mushrooms.

I even had my chakras tested by a guru during a weekend at an ashram, and *tried* the exercises he gave me to properly realign them.

All of these, I chose based on my own research and without consulting a professional. Why?

Because. Reaching out for help is something for other people. Me? I'm supposed to figure it all out on my own. Yeah…me…superwoman. Not!

I still haven't physically moved at all in my bed, still on my side, head on one pillow, one between my knees, one in my arms like an infant, and one scooched up against my sore back. The dog next door barks. Once. This catches my attention because she never barks; she's just saying hey, welcome back, I think. It makes me smile.

I know I have no interest in just surviving, existing. And the only way to have a real life is to cure myself of this incurable cancer. This, I know too.

But I also now know I've only been *trying*. Just jumping into an ocean of cure flotsam on the advice of ghostlike gurus in cyberspace.

The realization sends hope swirling inside my shroud of pain. It seeps into it from so many angles that my physical pain begins to dissipate. My stomach doesn't gurgle nearly as much; the headache is nearly gone, nausea abated.

I manage to turn over to my right side without my brain falling out of my head from the move. Then, onto my back. Reaching for the bed's remote, I raise myself up to a lounging position. Eyes closed, I feel a smile form on my face. My heart lifts a little, feeling around to see if it's safe to expand and project love into the mix of this new information.

Thinking back, I see how I've been playing with the myriad tools available for healing, keeping myself distracted from the awfulness of my situation, thinking I'm doing something about it, the whole while using them without believing they'll work.

Nausea rises in me again from having sat up, but it's milder now. I hear another dog bark, this time in the distance. A bird chirping. Ah, a helicopter flying, not above my house, but nearby. I notice that I'm noticing these things. Makes me realize I'm coming around; no noises had caught my attention during my time in purgatory.

Then, something I read comes to me; the answer to my own healing is in my hands. Each of us *knows* the perfect answer for us; it's as close as going within. A matter of *listening, feeling*.

Now, I had to listen like never before.

Much like Rosie, the robot maid on the *Jetsons* (before the reboot version), who simply cleaned what she was programmed to clean, I've been going about my health regimen like an automaton following a recipe with little forethought, except, like Rosie in the reboot version where she's now developed a bit of a mind of her own, I sometimes change ingredients halfway through, like starting on new supplements, or dropping others with little consideration of the effect on me. Of course, I'm getting poor results!

From now on, my every action, every decision must be steeped in clarity.

Take my broken body and spirit and divest both of the emotional junk clogging up the energy channels within me. Lace them with more love than ever.

My heart lifts, and its love expands farther into my energy field.

I'm going down. Down to the elemental level, as I've been attempting to do in meditation.

But for real this time.

With intent this time.

With faith.

Precision.

BELIEF.

It's only now, faced with choosing between death and doing more than just existing, that I realize I've been doing the work—but *without believing it will work for me*. I've been looking at all those things that could heal me as if they were a *come-on*, as my mother would say.

Without intent, she transferred her skepticism to me.

Did I not feel I deserve to heal? This mystery could be solved by going back, way back. And going deep, and even deeper.

Emotions live physically in our bodies; science knows it now. Exorcise the negative emotion in the part of the body that is ailing, and it heals; or, if healed through other means, never comes back. Simple, right? Yet, simple doesn't always equate to easy, as we know. It requires much internal work.

Soon, I'll realize I've never worked harder. Soon, I'll realize why my mother only tried things.

To heal, believing that the things I do actually work is necessary. I must believe in my worthiness to heal, believe I deserve for the chemo, supplements, medicinal mushrooms, cannabinoids, and meditations to work for me. They must all align to a common goal: healing me.

I must believe that healing is for me, too.

Then, something I once read comes to me: for a goal or dream to be achieved, one must first decide. Looks like I skipped that step. So, now, I must.

Decide I believe.

Decide it will work.

Decide to do what it takes.

Decide it's happening no matter what.

Decide to choose life.

Decide to *thrive*.

And with no fanfare, like when I turn on a light as I enter a room, a switch flips in my mind.

I DECIDE.

Yet, that's just the first step.

Because a decision to do, without taking action, changes nothing.

PART III

ENTER THE WOO-WOO

Yesterday's Woo-woo is Today's Mainstream

I believe that *based-on-science*, newly discovered treatments, the so-called woo-woo stuff of today, is the mainstream stuff of tomorrow. And tomorrow is, or nearly is, here in many instances.

Things we do and use every day started out being regarded as too out there to believe in, no matter the proof provided. Humans tend to mistrust anything new. It takes enough of us to believe in something to cause the snowball effect needed to sway others enough to shift consensus. We resist change because we fear risk and fear ridicule if proven wrong. But there's another reason why it takes so long for a new product that could save lives to make it to the marketplace.

We all know that washing our hands is important to prevent getting and passing on germs. However, a Hungarian physician, Dr. Semmelweis, who first proposed the idea in the mid-nineteenth century, could offer no acceptable scientific explanation for his findings, only anecdotal evidence. Other doctors took offense at the suggestion they should wash their hands. They mocked him because his ideas contradicted the recognized scientific and medical opinions of the time. Even though he could show a drop in mortality in maternity wards to less than one percent when the practice was put in effect.

By 1865, nearly twenty years after he first proposed that the washing of hands with a chlorinated lime solution in obstetrics saved the lives of mothers and infants, he'd become increasingly outspoken about his theory, but continued to be so ridiculed for his idea of handwashing that it caused him to suffer a nervous breakdown. That's when his colleagues removed him from their circle by having him committed to an asylum. While there, guards beat him, and he died fourteen days later.[1]

And yet, today, no doctor would dream of entering an operating room—not even an exam room—without first thoroughly washing his or her hands. Now, we all regularly wash our hands with soap even when there's no pandemic. Even those of us who aren't doctors.

Everyone knows that germs cause disease, but this, too, was once pooh-poohed by the medical community. Even before Pasteur came along, others brought forth the theory, only to be mocked and shunned.

---

[1] https://en.wikipedia.org/wiki/Ignaz_Semmelweis

Pasteur is more recognized for it because he was the first to conduct and document convincing experiments. But an archenemy—who had his own theory about what caused disease—spearheaded a movement of germ theory denialists (kind of like the climate change denialists of today)—which lasted throughout the twentieth century. During his lifetime, these denialists followed what Pasteur did as if he were the Pied Piper, except in his case, it was to laugh at him instead of becoming mesmerized by his theory and following him and his ideas.[2]

What's the first thing you notice when you stand in front of a hospital nursery, looking through the glass at all the babies? If you're like me, your eyes go to the incubators. We think nothing of this; we know a premature baby who might not have survived now will because of that incubator. But it took the US medical establishment about thirty-six years to recognize they could save the lives of premature infants by using incubators.

At the time, so ridiculed was the idea of incubators, along with Dr. Martin Couney, who brought the new contraption to the US from Germany in 1903, that the doctor was relegated to setting up shop at the famous Coney Island, New York, amusement park. There, people viewed the babies in their incubators for the price of twenty-five cents. The doctor used the money toward the care of the infants so parents wouldn't have to pay.

---

2. https://stmuscholars.org/germ-theory-of-disease/ and https://www.medscape.com/features/slideshow/medical-breakthroughs#page=8

He claimed an eighty-five percent success rate and is said to have saved 6,500 babies over forty years.

By 1943, because of his success, there were enough hospitals around the country with incubators that he was able to close the "show" at Coney Island. Not all that woo-woo after all, now, was it?[3]

History is riddled with such stories, so you'd think it would now be faster for a so-called alternative treatment with evidence to support it to move from woo-woo to what we call conventional treatment. Yet, in the United States, at least, it takes twenty years for such a treatment to be universally accepted.

Until the current thought leaders—who will always suppress upcoming thought leaders—retire or die off, upcoming thought leaders will have to fight to get their product into the marketplace. It currently takes about twenty years for a new [medical] product to make it in today's marketplace. I'm paraphrasing Brigham Buhler—owner of Ways2Well in Houston Texas, a clinic that offers what some consider controversial regenerative therapies—in an interview on the Joe Rogan show.

This is worth repeating in case you missed it.

Even in our quickly evolving world, *it takes twenty years for a new medical protocol to make it to mainstream marketplaces.*

This means that way before it becomes mainstream, a cure might already exist for diseases we still say are incurable.

---

3. https://en.wikipedia.org/wiki/Martin_A._Couney

And since I might not have tomorrow unless I do something today, I'm not at liberty to wait until the laughter dies down around whatever might heal me.

Thankfully, there are now more doctors who profess the benefits of combining Western and alternative medicine, calling it integrative, but they're still mostly being held on the fringes of conventional medicine, though this is changing fast, thankfully.

Dr. Andrew Weil, educated at Harvard, became internationally recognized as a pioneer of integrative and holistic health when he founded the Program in Integrative Medicine at the University of Arizona. In 1994. It took more than a decade after that for medical schools to begin to accept that perhaps integrative medicine has a role to play.

Other doctors, too, either following in his footsteps, or after a lot of soul searching and deprogramming themselves from what they learned in medical school, have moved on to, in addition to conventional protocols, touting the benefits of eating clean foods, and some even promoting *old-timey* healing remedies along with, or instead of, synthetic drugs.[4]

They, too, of course, are sometimes shunned by colleagues. But, not by anyone who hasn't found the answer in Western medicine to heal whatever ails them. Or those who, like me, have come to realize that integration assures the highest success.

---

4. https://www.healthline.com/health-news/alternative-medicine-becoming-mainstream

Yet, your health insurance covers none of these doctors' services or anything they prescribe ...

I don't want my life to be one of only visits to doctors, hanging with other people with this or that disease, to be the one who talks about nothing but her disease.

So, I forge my own path, and keep searching for what will cure me, not just keep me in what some might call the Big Pharma Ideal Patient club. To belong to the club, you must be a person having to take one of their drugs forever in order to stay alive.

The argument made by the alternative side of the fence for proving this "true," is that they can't make money if you're cured, and they can't make money if you're dead. So, therefore their business model must fall on mainly making drugs that keep you on the brink.[5]

Yet, during my healing journey, I've come to understand that, except for outliers, most scientists working for pharmaceutical companies, and those that run them, do want to find cures for the diseases they study.

Imagine the trifecta: cure, glory, more money.

A place in history as demigods.

Why would they not want that? I suppose they might not want it if, in the end, their success becomes their demise when they run out of patients to treat.

---

5. https://www.medpagetoday.com/opinion/revolutionandrevelation/72407

No matter what, though, their synthetic drugs alone aren't enough. The side effects of all current drugs require drugs of their own to manage, and those drugs require drugs of their own too, ad infinitum.

And this is good for the makers' bottom lines.

Really, the whole thing is a shitshow I can't overly contemplate if I'm to retain my sanity.

From a personal standpoint, though, I find it difficult to slam an industry whose products saved my life even if said products come with problems. Chemo wasn't enough to keep me one hundred percent healthy, but it DID keep me alive.

It's just that I got much better when I added alternatives to it. My quality of life became the same as before I got sick after adding them to my regimen in an intelligent manner, rather than haphazardly. I healed at a level that keeps the disease from coming back to take a bigger bite out of me.

All this just to prepare you for all the woo-woo stuff I will soon unleash upon you.

Everything I present here has scientific or solid anecdotal evidence to support it. Yet most of it is still relegated to the woo-woo cupboard up in the back of the attic—the cupboard that brings a lot of trepidation to the one who decides to open its door for the first time.

Some of the stuff behind the door requires a wide-open mind, and strong control over the rolling of eyes.

But those of us in my position have little choice in the matter. If we wish to survive, to thrive, we need to open that door wide and dig around in the cupboard, arms buried up to our elbows! I must do this, must live as if life guarantees me a tomorrow.

Groping Through the Darkness

"Well, you're resilient. I'll say that." Her hand already on the doorknob, she pauses, as if she's thought of something else. Finally, she adds, "Not always compliant, but definitely resilient."

I want to laugh but keep it down to a smile. She wears her own small smile but shakes her head back and forth slightly at the same time, like a teacher reacting to a somewhat naughty child. And then she heads out of the exam room after our monthly doctor-patient visit. Before that, it was weekly, then biweekly, now monthly.

The woman who delivered that message is the oncologist in charge of administering chemo treatments to me. There is also an oncologist who specializes in multiple myeloma and prescribes the treatment.

As far as I can tell, a large majority of people stop there when it comes to treating their multiple myeloma, or any cancer.

But, as the oncologist said, I'm not always compliant. At the beginning of treatment, I didn't take charge near as much as after The Night. That's when my noncompliant self began to take part in all our conversations, when I started to push back against the "standard of care" rhetoric dumped on me since the day of my diagnosis.

This was my first visit since The Night. I told her about that awful twenty-four-hour period, how I prayed for death, but ultimately decided to live and thrive instead. I explained that, to me, this means taking charge of my treatment, always asking her opinion and that of the multiple myeloma specialist, as well as that of the other practitioners and doctors about to come on board my train, destination Thriving. I won't do anything stupid.

You can't thrive if you're dead.

But I also will not blindly follow the generic protocol handed to every multiple myeloma patient.

Too often, we give away our power to the medical establishment treating us without questioning anything. We allow caretakers to make all our decisions for us. Allow our disease to dictate how every moment of our lives will play out.

This makes for a life lived under the control of others, which depresses us. It gives the disease precedence in our lives. It *becomes* our life instead of our life being affected by it. There is a difference.

When did we decide to give away our power like that?

This good doctor looked at me, shock on her face at what I'd gone through, but also fought me on a dosage reduction because I believe she truly believes that only chemo at that prescribed dosage will keep me alive; that anything else I do might make me think it will help, but that it does nothing.

In the end, I stood my ground and said that if dosage couldn't be reduced on one chemo drug, and the second drug that covers both multiple myeloma and breast cancer stopped completely, I'd leave her office and forgo chemo treatment altogether, taking my chances with the alternatives only. No hard feelings. I made it clear that I choose death over another similar twenty-four hours because of what I saw as a chemo overdose.

"If I can't have a life, I don't want to be here."

Her eyes large on me, she said nothing at first. She then turned to her computer and clicked around in there, her upper body leaning toward the screen, her eyes latched to it, face tense, as if intent on finding an answer. A minute or so later she turned back to me.

"Okay, I can lower the dosage on the one by twenty percent. And, okay, we'll drop the other…you'll have a mastectomy, so it could be all right to skip it if you really don't want it. But I don't recommend it."

Her shoulders slumped while relief coursed through me like a shot of Valium. One person happy, the other sad; no win-win here. I thanked her, told her I'd be doing a lot of other things to enhance the benefits of the chemo and to control its side effects.

"I found a naturopath oncologist and have an appointment with her next week. She already told me that she plans to order a bunch of tests, blood and stool, tests you can't do here."

She tried to keep a neutral face as her training no doubt taught her, but her eyebrows rose as if against her will, and her lips pursed. To her credit, she kept her eyes on me the whole time I talked, really listening. I appreciated that.

At the next visit, she holds in her annoyance at my explanations about the alternative treatments I now engage in, a protocol the naturopath oncologist devised for me. She does her best to listen patiently as I hand her the list of the numerous supplements I now take, the list devised after test results ordered by the naturopath came back. But I feel her distress, and, is that annoyance? I feel bad about the distress because I know she cares. I ignore it.

To thrive, I must focus on *my* needs, not on what another might think of my chosen way to address them.

There's no such task on the list of things to do to accomplish my mission of thriving.

In addition to the naturopath oncologist added to my Team Heal Maryse, there's now also an acupuncturist. And the technicians who set me up for red light treatments and infrared sauna treatments.

When put this way, it sounds like my life has been nothing but a series of doctor visits, taking fifty supplement pills per day, walking fifteen to twenty minutes after every meal (Yay! I get to listen to a book), getting poked by acupuncture needles, chemo needles, lying on cold and hard metal tables for diagnostic purposes in rooms frigid enough to preserve meat, sitting for long hours in infusion rooms, all of it creating an assembly line of sorts for my daily life.

Yet, there's been time to meditate for an hour each day, time to run my small business to pay the bills, time to spend time with family. Time to travel. Time to write. Time to read, read, read!

Time. It stretches or shrinks based on your perception of it. I live as one with plenty of it, therefore it appears. Meditation makes one realize that when one gets into the flow of anything one engages in, time seems endless, is endless.

Two weeks after The Night, I feel more vibrant than I have since my diagnosis three years prior. I am firmly walking out of the darkness and clearly see the bright path of my life journey just there ahead of me.

It's no time at all until both my feet are set firmly on it, but I find the path strewn with debris, small rocks, a few boulders to climb over.

Then, resistance sets in; doubt weaves its way through me.

Worst of all, apathy settles in, stubborn, with no plans to let go. Worse than trying versus doing, it turns out to be my true Achilles' heel. So, eliminating it comes first, ahead of the myriad other things to deal with on my healing journey.

Apathy

As they got older, my parents both did what their mainstream doctor told them to do, took all the pills prescribed to them, had all the recommended surgeries. Never explored healing any further.

Never got second opinions.

They also, my whole life, never discussed things of importance, and to me, their disinterest in those points to apathy. Me having run away from home at every opportunity beginning at age nine? Never spoken about; not back when I did it, and not after I became an adult. It simply was. Nothing to be done about it. Zero interest in why.

One of my brothers physically abusing the mother of his children until she felt compelled to go into a shelter with their three children? Never discussed, except for my mother once bitching about her grandchildren's mother having "done that to him," meaning to my brother. *He couldn't have hit her that hard*, she told me, and said nothing more. Might have had to do with the look of disbelief on my face regarding her attitude—but really, no surprise considering her own abusive behavior toward my siblings and me. Also, the fact that, the way she saw it, nothing could be done about this either. Just stare the event in the face, never feeling interested enough to make a move to fix it. Just try something; don't actually engage with it.

Truths surrounding our family dysfunction lay under the table like neglected dogs: kicked every now and then, like my mother mentioning my brother having hit his partner, but the foot kicking it quickly drawn back lest anyone in the vicinity start discussing the issue related to the cryptic comment about it, lest anyone do something about it. *Pass the relish* was much easier to handle than *Why do you keep running away like that? Why did his partner, a level-headed woman, think things were so bad that she had to go into a shelter with three children under the age of five?*

My parents watched life like one watches a TV drama; nothing's expected of the viewer. Their children, including me, caught the habit early as children naturally take on the habits of adults around them.

Through observation or osmosis, I learned at a young age to have no real interest in problems. You ignore them, or you pretend to do something about them while feeling no interest in them; that's all.

You allow this emotional fallout from neglect to bury itself so deep that it burrows into your subconscious, until you no longer even realize its existence. And there, feelings from the buildup of negative events fester. When the level of energy emanating from them gets too high for the nervous system to handle, you erupt.

The power company that shut the power off for most of three days in my area when it was six degrees Fahrenheit because the system was overloaded gets a good talking-to even if you're the only one who can hear it. You might even smack your tablet on the table so hard the screen cracks.

Once they reached their early eighties, both of my parents' health declined suddenly and rapidly. All the buried drama had finally built up so much in their bodies that serious illness ensued because that's what happens with emotional buildup. Like all energy—and emotions are energy—it eventually turns to matter once it builds up enough.

Both talked of their health issues almost exclusively yet showed no interest in fixing said health issues; they made no effort to find out the actual goings-on in their bodies. It was more like monologues on the list of tests they'd had and drugs they took. When asked what any certain ailment was, exactly, they'd only shrug in response.

To thrive, I certainly can't follow in their footsteps like a good little duckling.

I need to dig deep, find and erase all the pain of the past, the buried anger, shame, anxiety, and guilt, all of which only flare like fireworks at events that have nothing to do with what brought them on in the first place. Apathy has no place here.

I'd been in therapy for nearly three years before it surfaced that some of those fireworks come from displaced anger. That me flitting from one healing modality to another without believing it will work is simply a mechanism my psyche uses to distract me from the apathy that doesn't want to die any more than I do.

Were it not for The Night, I might never have realized that I approached all I did to heal more as play, as a distraction, than as real healing tools that could make a difference.

I *intellectually* believed in the healing protocols I engaged in but viewed them like something on an infomercial. I felt somewhat put upon when taking the supplements, the herbs, going to the infrared sauna, sitting down to meditate.

This must be overcome, and it starts with no longer playing with my healing modalities of choice, no more thinking, *Oh, this is cool, I'll try it for a while.* No. This trying of things is apathy's wingwoman keeping me occupied while I do nothing constructive. Just going round and round on the merry-go-round of pretense of *doing* while apathy does its thing of keeping me, well, apathetic, disinterested.

There is no try. And no half-ass doing. I now have this on a Post-it note on my bathroom mirror. Each morning I see it and am reminded that today, I Do. I not only try.

I must take it all on as if it were a life-or-death matter. Because it is. Apathy has no place here.

I resolve to look directly at anything I choose to do healthwise like it's a person standing in front of me. That person demands my attention, commands my respect. Leaves me no choice but to pay it heed, to act on its requests. Act on them mindfully, happily, with faith in the outcome.

I must address all aspects of my whole being to ensure my healing: mind, body, spirit. It must be done with assurance, belief, and faith like I resolved to do on The Night.

To overcome that early training by my parents requires a lot of self-control. Sometimes, I catch apathy doing its thing; my eyes travel to the vitamins and supplements on my kitchen counter and I think, oh, later. Even though I completely missed yesterday. When that happens, whether it's supplements, or meditation, or exercise, or making a new series of appointments with the acupuncturist or the naturopath, I'm forced to grab the scruff of my neck and gently guide myself over to the supplements, and to the phone despite a strong compulsion to do nothing.

Apathy puts up a good fight at times, but it isn't strong enough to overcome a woman who's chosen thriving over death.

Removing it from my energy field, from the fabric of my psyche, never ends because it keeps attempting comebacks.

First, I stop thinking of my illness as something I deserve to have happened to me. Instead, I resolve to think of it as something that should have never happened. If I deserve it, there's no compulsion to do anything to change it. This is another way apathy keeps itself alive.

Next, in a nonapathetic way, instead of reading all the contradictory information online about the best way to get as healthy as possible with multiple myeloma, and allowing myself to try those things like a hobby in which I have only a mild interest, I diligently follow the regimen given to me by the naturopath oncologist.

As promised, she orders a slew of medical tests—not covered by health insurance—and considered to not be needed by the current medical establishment. Woo-woo, in their opinion.

The results of the tests help my naturopath prescribe what is needed to help balance things out in my physical body. Do I lack Vitamin C? Do I show signs of inflammation? Where? Do I have the gut bugs that live on sugar (of course I do!)? What can I take or do to control the side effects of all these pharmaceutical drugs?

Her goal is to get my body back into balance and boost my immune system so it fights the invaders; it knows exactly how, but being depleted itself, it can only do so much.

Based on her recommendation, an acupuncturist, a physical therapist (because three years out from breaking it, my back still limits my motions—I can't even lie on it without a lot of pain when getting up), and various other health providers join Team Heal Maryse.

Still, apathy makes it difficult to move forward with intent and belief—constant reminders required—but the more I do it, the stronger I become, the stronger my resolve and the more the strings that tie me to it weaken and snap.

Overcoming apathy tops the list of what to do as one of the first steps on the road to Thriving.

With daily practice, as neuroplasticity promises, it fades away, replaced by a new habit.

I Do. I don't Try.

Stressing it Out

For the better part of twenty years, I ran a small business where my responsibilities included bringing in the money. The role required me to wear many hats, such as web development, writing all the copy for five websites, writing all the ads, marketing, writing, and keeping up with three blogs—and dealing with potential clients at one of the worst times in their lives. This caused me untold stress, especially after my diagnosis. And no doubt it helped cause my health issues.

Neuroscience states that stress affects brain function, which in turn causes physical symptoms, which in turn affect brain function, a merry-go-round of illness making, like high blood pressure, heart disease, obesity, and much more.

In other words, it's responsible for untold damage to the body, which holds no place in thriving.

I must eliminate it from my life on every possible level.

Leaving my business becomes one of my first challenges to overcome in my commitment to my new self. My old self argues. The business has been the largest chunk of my income for so long, how can I leave it behind? Doing so requires me to take a huge leap of faith that, after, the money will keep coming from other sources.

That alone could cause me stress. I feel stuck.

I can stay and continue to suffer the adverse effects of stress, for which I hit the mark on most symptoms.[1]

Or I can leave it, and my income, behind.

The constant stress over the responsibilities of running that business piles on top of the PTSD I suffered growing up, and which stayed with me as an adult, in addition to the PTSD incurred from my life changing so fast when I broke my back and was diagnosed, which initially sent me on a downward spiral, picking up angst, fear, sadness, and anger at the Universe on my way down.

And it appears that PTSD is a disorder that manifests as an improper negative response to stress. This leaves one unable to keep negative emotional responses within an acceptable range.[2]

I'm not the only one. The current state of the world causes many to suffer the negative effects of stress. And it goes a lot deeper than the annoyance of feeling it.

---

1. https://www.webmd.com/balance/stress-management/stress-symptoms-effects_of-stress-on-the-body#

2. https://www.ncbi.nlm.nih.gov/pmc/articles/PMC2882379/

It can affect the prefrontal cortex by taking it off-line, so to speak. Because it no longer communicates with the rest of the brain, it cuts off our ability to engage in thoughtful behavior. And it strengthens the amygdala in its tendency to engage in impulsive behavior, in knee-jerk reactions to situations. Sadly, *my* amygdala embraced such behavior, which served me well a few times but mostly hurt me.

Once I know all this, there's no way for me to justify remaining in my stressful business if being healed at one hundred percent is the goal.

Of course, no matter how vigilant, no matter how many changes I make, some stress will happen anyway because it's part of life. The problem is that, thus far, it's been not only a part of life, but *a way of life* for me. Its presence overshadows everything else to a point where I hardly know it's there.

How I perceive it can change immediately, therefore lessening it somewhat, though without forgetting that it's a stopgap only, just like applying a band-aid does nothing to fix the boo-boo it covers up. More must be done.

Rather than focus on its negative effects, I can acknowledge that, in certain situations, stress proves helpful. Just this one small change in perception can apparently lower my mortality by forty-three percent, according to neuroplasticity experts like Dr. Irena O'Brien.[3] Interestingly, after a stressful life event such

---

3. https://neuroscienceschool.com/

as I've had, it has also been shown that helping others lowers mortality by thirty percent.

In my old business we helped people, but at one of the most hostile times in their lives. Most appreciated our efforts greatly. But some of them turned into unreasonable, selfish, blaming beings, which sent my anxiety, and blood pressure, soaring.

So, months after The Night, I find a way to leave the stress of my business behind: I will leave the business behind.

I choose to have faith that things will work out, that the money will keep coming.

It's a good start, but hardly enough for someone who's lived in stress her whole life. More mind must be paid to how I feel at any time during the day.

If stress presents itself, I take deep breaths, relax my muscles so that the message that makes it to my brain is that there's no danger. No need for my brain to send messages to all my muscles and organs that danger's afoot, which over time fatigues my organs and damages my immune system.

I focus on something that calms me, like seeing myself on a beach, listening to waves flowing in and flowing out; I breathe to its rhythm.

Meditation helps.

Feeling grateful for what I have helps.

Spending quiet time with loved ones helps.

Deliberately feeling content helps.

I'm a Kintsugi Person

As synchronicity would have it, just a few days after deciding to thrive through life, to make changes to become better than before The Event, I come across an online article about a book, written by Candice Kumai, a chef. It's titled *Kintsugi Wellness: The Japanese Art of Nourishing Mind, Body, and Spirit*.

In it, she takes kintsugi, the Japanese art of putting back together pieces of broken pottery using a compound of resin and gold, silver, or platinum dust, making the pottery more beautiful than before the breakage. She marries this idea with mind, body, and spirit wellness. In other words, she suggests taking our broken selves and rebuilding them into better, upgraded versions, acknowledging our scars, be they spiritual, physical, or mental, and being proud of them rather than trying to hide them.

Considering where I'm at in life right now, the concept captures my imagination. Not only has my spirit been broken and needs rebuilding, but I also still have a mastectomy and breast reconstruction to go through, which will involve some ugly physical scarring on four different locations on my body. Why not, in the process, see more beauty in myself, inside and out, by adopting this concept?

I think of an incident, months earlier after the mastectomy. The doctor had given me the green light on exercising, and by then I'd made peace with losing my one breast. So, I'm on my back deck—visible from my neighbor's yard—wearing yoga pants, a tank top, and sports bra. A falsie to fill the place of my missing boob sits in my sports bra. I stretch my arms overhead in preparation for a forward bend and lean forward and down. Before my fingers can even reach my feet, the falsie falls out of my bra and plops onto the deck. Did the neighbors see? A quick glance says no; no one's outside.

First, shame and embarrassment come. Then, deciding that, who cares? This happened and so what; I see the humor in it. I laugh my ass off. I don't post this on IG, but I do share the incident with my children and with a few friends. We all have a good laugh. What could have been a stressed moment, a moment to increase sadness and anxiety, was made more interesting, and more uplifting, by seeing the humor in it. A bit like the new outlook on a piece of kintsugi pottery.

Why not acknowledge, embrace—flaunt, even—my emotional, mental, and physical scars? By lacing them with love into normality, into an unparalleled magnificence because of their uniqueness in the world, just like kintsugi pottery?

Because no one else can have the same since no one breaks in quite the same way, and I'm rebuilding from the aftermath of the ravages of the perfect storm that hit only me.

So why not lace the whole thing with love since precious metal isn't practical here?

Much later, after having been released from the hospital after the breast reconstruction, which takes place ten months after the mastectomy, I find myself unable to look at my chest in the mirror. It had taken me nearly three months to do so after the mastectomy.

But, one morning, I feel that something might be wrong.

There were issues with the reconstruction. The surgery involved removing two flaps of tissue and skin from the inside and back of my thighs, moving several veins and one artery too. Because things didn't go as planned, the procedure required two additional surgeries nearly back to back soon after the first, so all of me feels excessively vigilant, despite the miracle that occurred during the process, which I'll soon share.

I message the doctor's office.

The nurse asks me to send her a photo of the new breast to show the surgeon.

Take a photo? That means having to look at myself! Does she not realize this? Is she crazy?

I could just go to his office and let the nurse and doctor look at it instead, but it's forty minutes away from my home and this being a Monday, he's in surgery all day, so probably can't see me unless it's a true emergency. Hence the necessity of the photo; it will help him determine, as a first sign, whether the veins running through my new boob have failed again based on the color of the skin, among other things. If so, he'll have to readmit me for more surgery. Can't fool with this. Reverting to my old way of ignoring the signs could get me killed since I've been told that with no blood running through the veins, a septic infection could develop—which can quickly lead to tissue damage, organ failure, and death.

After her request for a photo, I head to my bed and recline for a while. The air conditioner hums. I hear the faint sounds of the dishwasher going through its cycles all the way across the house.

I raise the back of my bed and hear that mechanism going through its motions, too. Yup, the world seems to still be turning on its axis despite this awful task put before me.

That's when kintsugi comes to mind again. To embrace myself in this way necessitates looking at the thing. With humility, gratefulness that the wonder of modern medicine even allows for this procedure. Not with disgust and fear.

Reluctantly, I make my way to the bathroom. I think I'll take a photo in the mirror, but it's impractical because he just wants a photo of the boob, for one, and for another, no matter how I twist, my phone covers up the new boob in the image reflected from the mirror. A selfie with the self-facing camera is the only way, then.

Through slitted eyes, I look down at my phone as I lift my wifebeater-style top. Examining the new breast on my phone's screen instead of in the mirror, or by looking down at it, separates me from it. Checking in with myself, I realize that I feel neutral about it, which surprises me.

I examine it the same way I'd examine, well, a piece of kintsugi pottery, checking its gold or silver seams. I turn my head this way and that, staring at the new construction from different angles.

Objectively speaking, my new left boob is at the ugly AF stage.

Subjectively, I can't bring myself to hate it, to feel repulsed by it. I remember what the violent purple and yellow colors and the three wide, red, and deep scars of this new thing sitting on my chest like a piece of meat just plopped on there (because that's what it is) represent the road down which I've traveled, the one that's enriched my life beyond measure.

Being a real live piece of kintsugi isn't so bad, comparatively speaking.

How can I hate it when it's given me so much?

Reframing a Picture

On an early morning in July 2008, I got a call I'd been expecting. A few months before, a close friend, Danielle (fake name), had made me promise to go to her family's farm in Canada to say goodbye to her mother, Louise (fake name), before she exited life, if her illness came to that.

Danielle also wished me to be there to support her as she watched her mother transition. They'd been close, and she found the process difficult.

I knew Louise fairly well from visits to the farm in the past. Also, I'd seen her many times when she'd visited my friend in Las Vegas, and both mother and daughter had visited me in Arizona when I lived there (they were the friends, who, along with me, saw those cows on the golf course). Every Christmas, Louise sent me a greeting card with a letter in it, her handwriting tiny and leaning heavily to the left, making it a challenge to read, one I relished. In it, she'd describe everything going on in her life, and oftentimes, I found wisdom in there that applied to me. I loved that woman.

So, on that morning, I scrambled to find a flight to Montreal, one that would get me to the farm before Louise's arrival home the next morning. Danielle said that there was very little time left.

Louise arrived home in an ambulance, a hospice nurse right behind her, just a few minutes before I made it there from the airport, a sixty-minute drive away. She'd been taken off all liquids and nutrition. The EMTs placed her into a hospital bed brought into the first floor sewing room, made into a makeshift bedroom, so Louise wouldn't have to be transported upstairs on the narrow staircase of the hundred-year-old house.

My friend's two brothers were there, too, along with their own families. We all sat at the dining room table, a shroud of gloom over us all, conversation coming in fits and starts, mainly about practicalities, such as where's the kitchen scissors, or the dishwashing soap, and other such banalities. We took turns going into the bedroom to visit with Louise who rested in mostly a state of unconsciousness. I had a moment with her myself as I stood by the bed, holding her hand. Suddenly, she smiled at me, not just with her lips, but her eyes opened and had that familiar twinkle in them. That's when I cried for the first time.

Louise's impending death brought us all to her house to say goodbye. What had gotten her to that point was a disease none of us had ever heard of—a thing called multiple myeloma.

The family had been told that there was no cure. Before being brought home, Louise had spent the previous three months in the hospital. Back then, MM patients often experienced bone breakage, and the hospital kept her safer from that. Plus, as it gets closer to the end, patients' organs fail, so that had to be handled, too.

Louise passed peacefully at the crack of dawn the next morning, my friend at her side.

When I was diagnosed, it's the image of Louise's weak smile and twinkling eyes at the moment we connected that first came to mind. How could my brain go anywhere but to thoughts of her, to what she'd gone through?

After The Night, I come to realize that because of my experience with Louise, my psyche equates MM with imminent death being the only possible outcome, no matter how upbeat I try to remain, and no matter what I do to find a cure.

It hits me like a bolt of lightning! To survive, to thrive, I must reframe how I look at the situation.

All that about dealing with multiple myeloma during Louise's time is true, but it was twelve years ago. Plenty of people now live better and longer and experience a better quality of life overall despite dealing with MM. It's up to me, to anyone dealing with serious chronic disease, to decide to look at it differently.

I must remove the emotions and memories attached to what I know of multiple myeloma as it was twelve years ago. You see, that knowledge had embedded in me the belief that multiple myeloma means certain death.

I realize now that I can reframe this thing.

First of all—and this is my reframe—I now see it as a condition I live with, not one with an absolute outcome. I see it as a condition over which I have a modicum of control if I do the work to keep myself as healthy as possible. I see the opportunity to do so as a gift, considering that in Louise's time, multiple myeloma nearly guaranteed death to those afflicted.

Now, it still means that for too many, but 34% of patients make it as of the time of this writing, and that beats nearly no one making it at all. I choose to enjoy being part of the 34%.

How long I can treat it before I no longer can is up to too many factors to mention. Staying on top of new treatments, taking care of my immune system, ridding myself of the negative garbage in my emotional body, and going into Nothing during meditation to bring back health, among other things, come to mind.

But, I now deal with how I view the situation from the perspective of, not imminent death, but of simply a challenge turned teacher in my life.

I've reframed the picture and it looks a whole lot better now.

Just Breathe

Around age twelve, I learned how singers breathe: take air in all the way into the belly and slowly release it through my vocal cords to form sounds. My father, a singer himself, taught me. For reasons unknown to this day, I chose to be above that. I'd be the one who didn't visibly inhale while singing; and, later, as I talked, too, just generally as I went through my day.

This continued even after my father told me the story of how, after he'd stopped singing professionally, he'd begun to get migraines and couldn't figure out why, nor could his doctor. Somehow, one day, he realized that he'd gotten into the habit of taking in only shallow breaths. From the day of that insight, he committed to inhaling deeper and to check himself many times during the day, especially when he felt a migraine coming on. They disappeared.

Now, why would a twelve-year-old girl think she can belt out a song by doing the very opposite of what she needs to do to make it happen? No idea; just know she did it. I can't even take ownership of that crazy idea; I turn it over to some generic "she." So, I trained myself to get along without the very thing we all need for our health (and singing voice) to flourish.

And of course, my singing voice became this thing that put my body through distress since singing requires breath on which to glide. That's why Celine Dion is Celine Dion, and I'm the one who just sings in the car and in the shower.

To add dichotomy to this, at age thirteen, I learned deep belly yoga breathing, but saw it as something to calm myself in moments of panic, as something to do when in distress only, an exercise to engage in behind closed doors. When I remembered. The rest of the time? This girl would show the world she could do it all.

Without breathing.

Oy...the mind of a child...

Watch your children closely. Even with your eyes fully on them, they're concocting some nutso idea about how to be. With five kids in the house and two working parents, no one noticed that most of the time, I barely inhaled.

This resulted in short, shallow breaths that just managed to keep me alive. Alive, but not well. This habit of mine continued until the recent past when it was high time to do something about it.

We don't think about breathing much, except perhaps as a twelve-year-old who decides to minimize her own. Our bodies delegate this crucial act to our parasympathetic nervous system, so it takes some doing to change how one does it.

In my perennial search for what might heal me, with my new resolve to address each issue that affects me with mindfulness, an audiobook titled *Breath: The New Science of a Lost Art* shows up in the feed on the app where I buy audiobooks, as if the Universe knows I need it. The author, James Nestor, attributes all sorts of health issues to shallow breathing, such as anxiety, high blood pressure, and more. Shockingly—or not—I suffer from both. He also states that autoimmune disorders can be helped with proper breathing. Several studies link multiple myeloma and its precursor, monoclonal gammopathy of undetermined significance (MGUS), to several autoimmune conditions, though more studies are needed to confirm it.[1] But do I have time to wait for that?

So, I listen, and discover that most of us breathe incorrectly. We either take in shallow breaths spaced far apart (my old habit) or we take shallow breaths, very fast, in and out.

Learning to breathe properly on the regular and doing deep breathing exercises every day will help heal my anxiety, depression, high blood pressure, and cardiac irregularities, which I sometimes experience. Those who engage in proper breathing experience improvement in general health and an increase in energy.

---

1. https://www.ncbi.nlm.nih.gov/pmc/articles/PMC4900299/

I'm not even halfway through the book before I go online to find a man mentioned in the book, Wim Hof, a well-known breathing teacher, but someone I've never heard of. When his wife passed away years ago, he dove into yoga to deal with his grief. This led him to discover pranayama, a form of yoga breathing that calms and energizes the mind and body. He also engaged in Tummo, a form of breathing meditation practiced since ancient times by Tibetan monks. This led him to create his own breathing method—albeit without Tummo's religious overtones.

The first things I notice after a few days of doing the exercises he leads online, and consciously paying attention to my breath the rest of the day, are a drop in blood pressure (high blood pressure being a side effect of the various chemo drugs administered to me for more than two years), next to no anxiety, and improved concentration. I'll take it.

Thousands of people claim to have been helped through Tummo breathing as well as by the Wim Hoff method. Their YouTube videos are worth a listen.

This might not heal me of cancer, and it doesn't claim to, but it enhances my quality of life greatly and gives my body something that, at a minimum, it needs to flourish rather than flounder. It also helps my emotional body as anxiety and depression start to disappear.

I also feel more energetic, high almost, and the afternoon slump that's often slowed me down no longer shows up. When my back locks up, as it still sometimes does, deep breathing brings it back to normal faster.

The reason for breathing properly is that it oxygenates our bodies and gives our cells something they need to thrive. I'm exploring getting even more oxygen into my body via hyperbaric chamber treatments. At this point, there's evidence that this helps patients about to undergo a stem cell transplant (one treatment offered to MM patients) because it weakens the multiple myeloma cells before the initial chemo treatment associated with the transplant is administered. There are studies going on right now, but no results yet as of this writing.[2] There's also no evidence that it helps outside of a transplant, so I'm holding off, but watching carefully. Once the MM cells have been weakened, something has to happen to get them to die. We don't want them weakening and then somehow becoming reenergized; no point to that.

But, even if at some point multiple myeloma comes back in a rage over having been banished from my body, I'll want to enjoy what life is left in me, and breathing properly helps. I'll want to spend my last days surrounded by my loved ones; to talk to my granddaughter about her plans for the future, warn her about bad boys (enjoy them; don't make long-term plans with them), help her plot her escape from the mundane, and encourage her

---

2. https://clinicaltrials.gov/ct2/show/NCT04862676 and https://www.cancer.gov/about-cancer/treatment/clinical-trials/search/v?id=NCI-2020-08169

to live her life in such a way that she can say at the end, "I'm goin' in style!" just like her Mémé (her name for me).

I'll extract a promise from my son to love himself more, to forgive himself for sins he committed and those he thinks he committed. One from my daughter to continue on her path to living her best life however that looks to her, regardless of what others might think of it.

We should all take our last breaths surrounded by love, by the certainty that we gave this life our all, that we are happy to be moving on to wherever the Universe takes us when we leave here.

Meanwhile, let's breathe on and thrive!

On Friendship

There's a new breed of Instagram posts that point out the importance of dropping friendships that do not serve us and never have. Anytime a new one pops up on my screen, I cringe over how many people might be permanently blocking friends, canceling them over small disagreements because it's now hip to do that. Just because we don't agree with our friends one hundred percent doesn't mean the friendship should be tossed into the trash like yesterday's leftovers.

Finding a good friend is a bit like finding a rare painting at a flea market; they shouldn't be thrown out because of a little dirt or a nicked frame.

But, sometimes, we must.

I had a friend whom I considered family. Leslie (name changed to preserve her privacy) and I met when we were both going through a divorce. For years, we raised our children together, and went on more adult outings than I can count when the children were with their respective fathers. We shared our joy, our angst, our plans for a better future. We even shared a babysitter.

She sometimes treated me to her designer clothes and the occasional five-star restaurant dinners. She kept me laughing deeply into many evenings with jokes and her general joie de vivre. When she walked into a restaurant, a store, an event, and dang, even into a nail salon, all heads of not only men but also women swiveled her way, such was the strength of her presence, her personality.

She remained my friend for more than twenty-five years. When would you not want a friend like that? One with such a huge generous presence?

You wouldn't want a friend like her if the package included mood flips like hers. That's when.

One Thanksgiving, my son, Paul, then in his early twenties and living in Dallas, had flown in for the holiday. Leslie and I were celebrating at her house that year (we, and our children, always spent that holiday together). Paul had somehow gotten a severe ear infection between the time he left Dallas and the time he landed in Las Vegas. Lying on her sofa, he suddenly turned to his side and vomited. She began screaming the instant the first upchuck left his mouth. Screamed that he ruined her floor (it was tile), screamed I was irresponsible for not having cleaned it up the instant it landed on the floor. All this before Paul even finished.

I took him to the hospital and then to my home instead of back to hers. She didn't call to find out how he was doing; just left me a nasty voice mail a few days later about what a crappy friend I was for allowing him to vomit on her floor, and to have ruined the Thanksgiving dinner after all the cooking she'd done.

When our children were all under the age of ten, she talked me into allowing her mother, just then visiting from out of the country, to come stay with me for a while because Mom didn't like Leslie's boyfriend, and he'd moved in with her just before Mom arrived. Two months later, at my wit's end with Mom's unpredictable behavior—so similar to her daughter's—I called Leslie and told her I was bringing Mom back to her house.

Her response? "Don't you dare bring that woman to my house!"

Her pronouncement took the breath right out of me.

By the next day, nonetheless, at my insistence, Mom was back with her daughter. And daughter didn't speak to me for weeks.

The above are just two examples of many such meltdowns over the years, years during which I took many "Leslie breaks," as I called them

The last straw is when, after my diagnosis, while I'm dealing with the illness, the numerous doctors' appointments, while still shaky on my walking legs, my back sometimes still giving out, my mind often struggling to surface above chemo brain fog, she texts to tell me I better stay away from her family, or I'll have to deal with her. I've done nothing that should offend her to that point. Based on my years of experience with her, I know that, within a week, she'll invite me to lunch or dinner, all forgotten on her part—and that I'll never get an explanation for the outburst.

But *I'll* be dealing with emotional waste from it.

Unbeknownst to her, however, not long before, I began to clean out my Contact List. I resolved to be done with unreliable friends, friends who caused me angst, who didn't support me, who took and never gave, on whom I couldn't rely in moments of crisis. I reason that having five good, reliable friends of like mind, with whom I can share without fear of reprisal, will serve me, and them, better than dozens of friends who contribute little to the relationship, and who were of no help at a time I desperately needed it. "Sisters" who said "Love you" all the time, but disappeared when I lay on a hospital bed with a broken back and a death sentence hanging over me. The most difficult to deal with, though, is the not knowing when a friend will do a flip and attack like a treacherous fox.

So, sadly, I cancel Leslie.

Pain from doing this comes from the fact that she didn't disappear when I got sick; as a matter of fact, she sent food, brought food, sent money, helped out in the very early days when I refused to go to the hospital by badgering a doctor she knew into giving me a pain pill prescription after a telehealth visit only (before telehealth visits were the norm), something that might have compromised him, and her, both at risk of losing their professional licenses, or at least being sanctioned. She was *there* for me.

But, because it takes me days to get over her not-so-nice unpredictable actions and comments, and I never know when she'll next explode, it forces me to choose between her friendship and my well-being. By now, I meditate more often, make lists of what I want to do with my possibly limited lifespan. Living stress-free takes precedence over almost anything.

The debris from her breakdowns takes up too much space in my head: space I can use for more pleasant, and more productive, endeavors. At this point, I also come to realize that, when around her, I constantly edit my behavior, don't say certain things, stay perched on a ledge neither side of which looks attractive because no matter on which I fall, I'll be faulted. Too many other, more important things are happening in my life to allow for ledge balancing.

So, I carefully move off the ledge, lower myself to the couch, reach for my phone, and block her on all social platforms, on email, phone, and text. After, I stare straight ahead at the fireplace in front of me, focusing as sadness and lightness intermingle in my body, flowing into one another as rivers do at points where they intersect.

She's an extreme example of friends I let go; there are others, some with no more fault than being shallow friends that take up precious time that's better spent elsewhere.

Now, when I go back to Las Vegas to visit, other than my daughter, from out of a few dozen friendships and acquaintances, I can count on one hand those I make an effort to see. They're the friends of like mind, the ones with whom conversations invigorate me. And the ones who stepped up when I needed it while lying in a hospital bed, unable to move, twenty pounds underweight, and drugged up like some street corner addict. Except for the ones that, like Leslie, cause too much strife to bear.

To me, a better Instagram post on dropping friendships would read this way: "If you automatically surround yourself with an invisible shield each time you interact with 'that' friend, it's time to let her go like that favorite pair of jeans too full of holes and irreparable seams to save. The other friends, occasional disagreements or not, you keep."

More Shedding

Of all the so-called woo-woo stuff I come across, the most promising to me is fixing things at an elemental level, going where the negative emotions hold court in my energy field and in my body, and banishing them, with love, with persistence. This isn't easy, but I have to just do it, as the Nike tagline so famously says.

We have three levels of being that affect our health: mind, body, spirit. I determine to address all three at that primordial level.

Fix things there and allow the fix to morph its way through everything in my life. Everything. This means discard, discard, discard, until I find myself in unfamiliar territory, emotions-wise, and in my surroundings. Persist until the sought-after unfamiliar becomes the familiar, until it becomes my new normal.

The business that stresses me out so?

Less-than-true friendships where I must "prove" something?

Too many possessions requiring too much care and maintenance?

Holding in what should be said out loud?

Putting up with disrespect just to keep the peace?

Taking on more than I want, more than I can handle, just to show up in the world the way it wants to see me?

Saying yes when I want to say no?

Shed, shed, shed! Without The Event and The Night, the likelihood of me going there mindfully, acknowledging that true harm was done to me, that emotional trauma in its various residences in my body is a real thing? That it's the cradle of the turmoil in my life? No chance.

In time, I will have gone within deeper than ever, gathered the wisdom, and taken it back out with me. The reward? Loss of anxiety, anger, shame, guilt, and fear over *what others have done to me* (yes, this is a thing), and the unearthed benefit of newly found peace.

We've all been at the top of the world for moments in our lives. Imagine *living* there most of the time. Interestingly, to live in this rich environment doesn't require a five-thousand-square-foot house to lose all your stuff in, diamonds, pearls, or astronomically priced artwork on the walls. Nor does it require a "smart" car that costs the price of a house.

It just requires you to shed the baggage of past mistakes, shed people who do nothing to uplift you as you do them, shed the expectations of the world that don't parallel your deepest desires, shed the demands you place on yourself despite them not aligning with what you truly want.

That's all.

When we embrace and feel grateful for all we already have, a five-hundred-seventy-one-square-foot house with all our favorite comforts suddenly seems more luxurious than that twenty-seven-hundred-square-foot house with all the stuff society expects us to have, but that we left behind. An older car, kept well, feels brand-new. Restringing that ceramic flower bracelet instead of throwing it out and buying a new one feels joyful and empowering. Taking a seed from a lemon, planting it, and finding we suddenly have a lemon tree growing in that terracotta pot by the front door brings joy and increases our self-confidence in knowing we could survive without a supermarket, if need be; we now know we can grow food from so little.

The morning hour of self-care we allot ourselves for Morning Pages while drinking matcha, followed by twenty minutes of yoga, before we allow the world to intrude lends an air of luxury to the day; no stress, just bliss.

Anything feels new when we focus entirely on it with gratefulness in our hearts.

Thriving doesn't mean having to singlehandedly manage every little detail for things we believe will help in our goal to flourish. Take me, for instance. I want more than a lemon tree. I want a whole garden, but don't want to take care of a garden. Yet, I see myself in one, pulling weeds, or harvesting what I've sown; bloated-from-juice tomatoes, bright green beans, carrots pulled from the ground, radishes with their delicious greens, eating what I've grown. When I visualize that, my blood pressure lowers, my whole body relaxes, I feel the joy of being alive in my heart. That peace, that contentment that comes over me when I engage in activities that create such feelings? That's thriving to me.

Alas, having my own garden means curtailing my desire to travel far and wide for months at a time—another aspect of my idea of flourishing. So, instead, I volunteer a few hours a month at a small local farm that grows organic vegetables and fruits. I get to blossom in this area of my life while helping a farm that might not be able to survive without its volunteers. The feeling of gratitude, of well-being I get in return—not to mention fresh-from-the-garden veggies—is impossible to buy anywhere at any price. I've shed the garden while still gardening.

My father always said that we descended from Vikings—yes, I know they were barbarians in battle. But what a lot of people don't give them credit for their well-organized system for community and living, right down to the first parliament in history. Yin and yang applies here.

They were also mainly nomads, and I'm certain that DNA passed right down to me. I can't stand not going on a trip somewhere at least three to four times a year. I did it even as a very young person, starting as a teenager. The only years I sat still at home, with just one trip or so per year, was while raising my children. Unlike now, at the time, the world wasn't organized for families with school-aged children to travel for several months at a time. Plus, there were other family complications involved. Were I raising them now, they'd have experienced life in several countries by age twelve.

To me, there is no thriving without traveling. And unlike my Viking ancestors, my soul also needs a permanent home even if I only spend half the year there. To satisfy my need for a home, for travel, for a garden—because for me, they mean thriving—the Goddess of Creativity had to be called down to lend a hand.

By now, I've sold my large home in Las Vegas and moved to the Dallas area to build a tiny (to me) home on a property my son bought with the intent to build a family compound. Shedding that large, high-maintenance home alleviates some stress, too.

Several months after The Night, I leave the business that sustained me for many years. This means giving up my largest source of income. Plus, it allowed me to set my own hours, to work from anywhere and call the shots. But the stress eclipsed all benefits.

The relief, when I hand it down to a young lady starting out in the world of business, can probably be seen from Mars. She's all gung-ho to take it on, and I'm all gung-ho to let it go. A perfect match. Swipe right.

I have faith that money will keep coming for all my needs, that many more trips are coming my way, that I'll spend many hours of bliss in that garden, that fixing many more things instead of buying new ones will keep bringing me pleasure, and that for many years to come, I will cherish my small but exquisite home waiting when I return from indulging my Viking bone.

All this to say there's more than one way to thrive, and there's no need for millions of dollars to achieve it either. Our thrive paths are different: mine isn't yours, and yours isn't mine, or anyone else's. Thriving isn't a destination with only one road on the map to get to it; it's how to live consciously and joyfully on the way to reaching our goals. It's figuring out how to live creatively, how to get what we want in unorthodox ways, if need be, like satisfying my desire for a garden.

And shedding all surplus.

Doing all of this helped, but really, shedding in order to thrive requires a lot more than discarding baubles and houses and people. One must go much deeper within to shed the intangibles that cause more damage than the above.

One must go deep into the psyche, to dig out the rotted energy festering there. Fear of facing it has me still only at the mental exploration stage.

Trippin' Out of My Mind

No, I'm not talking about getting high on hallucinogenics. They're making a strong comeback in the field of psychiatry but because of *the side effects* of the high, not for the high itself.

And, okay, in addition to taking medicinal mushrooms in powder form, I microdose mushrooms—the psilocybin kind—for those side effects. There, I admit it.

Microdosing doesn't make you high at all. Still, there's controversy about its efficacy based on some recent studies (as in all new therapies, especially alternatives), but there's no denying what I feel, what it does for me.

Studies are ramping up again after having been banished into the dark in the early 1970s. We all know about Timothy Leary and his infamous studies during the '60s into lysergic acid diethylamide (LSD) in the treatment of mental health.[1]

Unfortunately, during that time, LSD was snuck out of labs at Harvard and the offices of psychiatrists. The emerging counterculture lost no time using it to get high, as a way to see God, some said, rather than to banish whatever mental illness might be meandering about their brains.

What didn't help matters is that Leary and his partner in the experiments, Richard Alpert, used the substances themselves and didn't follow the rules set by Harvard all that closely. You might know Richard Alpert as Ram Dass, what he renamed himself after his departure from the university.

In the end, the powers that be decided that Timothy Leary and his ilk were out to corrupt our youth; they did not want these drugs loose in the world. A conspiracy theorist might say that the people who run the world didn't want the small people to become enlightened.

At the same time, President Nixon declared a war on drugs. Before all this, though, the CIA and the US Army conducted many experiments with it, real cloak-and-dagger stuff.

Harvard eventually fired Timothy Leary. He was later arrested for smuggling less than half an ounce of marijuana from Mexico to the US. Some reports say he was given a thirty-year sentence, but he was arrested again two years later and given

---

1. https://dash.harvard.edu/bitstream/handle/1/41647383/Timothy%20Leary%E2%80%99s%20Legacy%20and%20the%20Rebirth%20of%20Psychedelic%20Research.pdf?sequence= 1

a ten-year sentence, so who knows. A report has him escaping prison and being found a few years later in Afghanistan. Nixon once called him the most dangerous man in America.

Anyway, due to all this controversy, research funding for the effects of psychedelics on the diseases that affect the mind went poof.

Microdosing is about as far as I go these days. No falling for the promise of ayahuasca either for me, no psychedelic trips of any kind. I'm not in it for the high, but for the benefits of alleviating anxiety, for the increased creativity, for focus on what I'm visualizing about my new life and in my writing. And microdosing enhances everything I visualize.

Out of my mind comes the visualization of me traveling the world without fear of needing constant medical treatment. In it, I no longer see an oncologist at all because there have been zero signs of any cancer in me for a long time. No visits to an infusion room. I don't even know what an infusion room looks like anymore.

I live in my pied-à-terre in the US, a small home that contains everything I consider important in a home, not the least of which is a wet room with a deep soaking tub in the bathroom; a fourteen-foot-wide closet with lights that turn on when the doors slide open, drawers with glass fronts so I can see what's in them, jewelry drawers, special drawers for my unmentionables, sliding shelves for shoes...you get the picture.

Some of these things have already manifested in my real life, some are well on the way to happening.

A microdose of psilocybin mushrooms alleviates the anxiety I've lived with all my life, and with which often comes depression, another emotion that blighted so much of my childhood that I'd accepted it as just another aspect of life and didn't even consider myself depressed; not that I'd have had much of an opportunity to discover it because, in those days, depression was only spoken about in hushed tones while the kids were out of the room. An older cousin had been admitted to a psychiatric hospital because of it, but I had to discover that fact by eavesdropping.

Microdosing relegates those emotions to my past, dissolves them from my present. I feel as if I am floating above the quagmire of the cancers using my body as their home, as if they're just something I'm thinking about instead of something in my reality. My surroundings are shinier, brighter, without blinding me.

I live like any vibrant woman of my age does—well, maybe not all women. Too many focus on acting the way society expects a woman of their particular age to act. Me? I don't use an *age gauge* when choosing activities.

Curtis Jackson (aka 50 Cent), in his memoir *Hustle Better, Hustle Harder*, says we all pay attention to the age the calendar says we are, the one based on our birthday. Instead, we're better off paying attention to today.

"Age isn't about the year you were born, it is about how you approach this year right now," he asserts.

So, in my mind, living in the age of today, I go zip-lining, unafraid that I'll break a bone, break my back again. I'm dancing the night away at an EDM concert, traveling the world with just one small suitcase as is the trend with digital nomads. I've developed friendships with people younger than I, calendar-wise, and those in my age group who embrace the world where it's at now rather than where it was at in the decades of our youths.

Through experience, I *know* visualization works. And now realize it works even better with microdosing. Progress!

So, if you can't go somewhere in real life yet, or ever at all, why not simply take yourself there in your head? I read that once something in our mind becomes more real to us than what's in our current reality, there is no doubt that, in time, it will occur for real. That once our brain believes an event has already happened, it causes us to accept the possibility, and to think of ways to make it happen in the three-dimensional world since the brain can't accept the dichotomy of it being real in our minds and unreal outside of it.

Placing myself in my future through enhanced visualization (via microdosing) makes me think of space travel without the danger. You can travel eons beyond your current reality and feel confident about making it back to our three-dimensional world.

While traveling, you are free to explore anywhere you wish. No borders, no customs agents. No immigration. The only thing that might stop you is you.

As another helpful and pleasant side effect, I notice that, at first only on microdose days, then on all days, it enhances my meditations, takes me deeper in.

My preferred way is to go as deep into my subconscious as possible—into blackness, into Nothing—where all possibilities exist.

The first few times I try to venture out with my feelings beyond a self-made energy barrier that I didn't notice during months of previous meditations, I hang back on its edge for a few seconds. Fear rises, so I pull back and keep on this side of it until the end of my meditation. It takes a few more tries before I surrender and let myself go into the Unknown beyond my self-made boundary.

When in that space, up and down disappear, side to side disappears, time disappears, my body disappears; I am all consciousness; awareness.

Because all possibilities for my life are there for the taking, I enter the field with the intent to come back one hundred percent healthy. Just like bringing back a souvenir for a loved one when on trips. I'm the loved one in this case. Because, with certainty, it's for me, too.

So, several times a week, I'm *tripping* away, in my own way. No need for psychedelics except in doses too small to get high. (I hope this doesn't disappoint too many of you!)

Still, just ridding myself of the symptoms of stress, anxiety, and depression won't fix things permanently unless the reason for feeling those in the first place is addressed. I'm nearly ready now.

Meanwhile, I enjoy creating a new life in my mind to manifest it outside my mind.

Health Freak

My foray into exploring ways to keep my body healthy started in my mid-twenties, especially after my son came into the world. I began to pay attention to nutrition, to supplements, to additives in food, to exercise, to thinking about meditation. I went for the whole natural birth thing until the last two hours, when I screamed for drugs, my labor totally off the Lamaze charts.

The health food bug stung me deeply. Enough that I made my babies' food myself because the ingredient lists on commercial baby foods at the time made the hairs on the back of my neck stand straight up.

Some years later, I read a cookie recipe that called for soy milk (this is before we all came to realize that soymilk plays havoc with our hormones). I resolved to make the soy milk myself. Off I went to the health food market to buy soybeans, which I soaked in water and some flavorings for several days. I then extracted the milk by squeezing the whole concoction through a nut milk bag. Oof. The cookies were gone in a flash compared to the amount of time it took me to make them. That's when I realized I might be going a bit too far and plopped myself on the couch with a good book and a one-pound bag of high-fructose corn syrup licorice, then a reward food for me. I'd soon revert to my healthy ways after such a *crise* (French word for tantrum), but another episode always loomed in my future because I chose not to look too closely at this pattern.

I tried out various exercise regimens, dreamt of self-sustainability while reading *Mother Earth News*, and believed I did all possible to keep my child, and myself, healthy. My then-husband and I looked for land in Oregon, though this never materialized.

Years went by and my quest for a healthy body continued as I paid attention to anything new coming out that pertained to antiaging. All for my body, though. I did nothing to address the emotional carnage life had sent my way early on, having been raised in a high-anxiety, physical and sexual abuse environment.

It was only after being diagnosed with breast cancer the first time at age thirty-eight that I discovered that emotional health, or rather a lack thereof, creates untold chaos in our physical bodies. *Emotional health? That's a thing?* I thought then.

But as we all know, there's a chasm between knowing about a thing, even an important one, and doing something about it. Especially when apathy lives in you.

As Steven Covey says, I was taking care of the Important and Urgent stuff such as being a single parent to two younger children, work, household chores, relationships, chasing the dollars necessary to support the whole show. And leaving the Important but not Urgent stuff, like my health, on the back burner to simmer and build up into Stage I breast cancer, then twenty years later into a cancer that nearly felled me. And for good measure, a repeat of breast cancer.

After my first breast cancer diagnosis, surgery, and radiation treatments, I sought alternative ways to deal with the stress and trauma of being diagnosed with cancer while a ten-year-old and four-year-old counted on me.

I flirted with meditation, and flitted about from health trend to health trend, totally directionless, a hummingbird who'd lost its radar.

I'd resolve to "get healthy" on Sunday, and on Monday morning I'd exercise, stop eating those *reward* foods, force myself to smile to uplift the dark moods that rose from the depths of my damaged psyche, try to sleep more.

Yes, I made all these changes at once. So, of course, I never stuck to my new routine for very long.

About four times per year, I'd put myself through this "new beginning."

Guilt followed the quitting of each new health routine. This behavior caused me more emotional damage, piling itself up on top of what already permeated every inch of the fabric of my being, like a shirt steeped in black tea.

I now know that not only was my emotional body damaged by early trauma, but that this trauma had found its way into my physical body, specifically into my left breast, then into my spine, and festered there, causing slow-moving chaos.

Looking back, I realize that it's only after a multiple myeloma diagnosis soon followed by a breast cancer diagnosis that I took my emotional health seriously. Realized that the constant guilting over not doing, or no longer doing, and treating myself to *reward* foods, and allowing the long train of negative thoughts winding its way around my mind day in and day out, contributed to the multiple myeloma diagnosis and to the repeat of breast cancer.

A mind is like a small child. Left unsupervised, it wanders. Wanders right into treacherous territory where land mines of negativity await the opportunity to blow up good thoughts and the matching feelings that follow. My adult self must supervise its meanderings, keep it on a positive path.

In *The Untethered Soul*, the author, Michael A. Singer, suggests we watch ourselves think for a while. He equates many of our thoughts to crazy talk from an unhinged roommate. He argues that, and I'm paraphrasing, if we lived with such a roommate, we'd kick them out pronto, or run away from home.

After doing this exercise for a few days, I must agree with him. My *roommate* goes from thoughts of my demise to thoughts of living in my Ideal Home, to thoughts of my son dying in the Ukraine, where he has been as a Ukrainian Foreign Legion volunteer—and Russians had found and begun to bomb training camps, one of which he'd been at just before the bombing. *Is he coming back?* Then, it goes to where we'll spend next Christmas as a family, to revenge thoughts toward my children's stepmother, who made life miserable for them while growing up. Then, my *roommate* wants to sell everything I own, buy a camper van, and hit the road. This, despite the fact I'm in the middle of a construction project on a house for me to live in.

All this crap in my head clutters up the real estate in there, overtaking positive thoughts. Nothing but disconnected *mind junk* spewing out of monkey mind.

And that's gotta go. Because I don't see it anywhere on the drop-down menu under Thrive.

During that fateful night when I chose Life, when I chose Thriving over dying, is when I *knew* I'd only understood things about my emotional health on an intellectual level. Not on an emotional level where it needs to be understood so I connect with it. Under the hood I needed to go.

After much research and reading on the subject, I come to understand that physical disease starts in our emotional bodies. And that our thoughts are what create the emotions. If you could have read my mind in the first third of my life, you'd see how I ended up with a serious disease despite my mostly clean diet and lifestyle (excepting the licorice, of course).

To fix this, I need to go where few human beings have gone before, to play on the now well-known words from *Star Trek*.

Cleaning out My Emotions

I'm about to go for a walk in the park behind my house. After months of rain and bipolar temperatures, it's sunny, it's warm, and no wind. But I can't find my fave cap to shade my eyes from the bright sun. I *know* it's somewhere on the shelf at the top of my closet, but can't see it, can't even feel it when running my hand along the shelf, over and around handbags. The two inches in height I lost when I broke my back does help because it keeps me from being able to reach back far enough.

I'll have to take a closer look. I drag a chair over and stand on it while I reach to the very back of the shelf. Ah, there it is, crammed far into a corner.

As I've said, negative emotions, especially the ones created by trauma, pick a spot in our bodies and hide there. Like my hat, they're not missing; they're just not visible.

You'd think that they'd fade away as the angst of the trauma diminishes, but no. Instead, if not eliminated, they grow in density when other similar events cause the same negative emotion, which finds its way to it (like energy attracts like). This buildup of energy eventually becomes matter in the form of disease. Science now knows that all matter comes from energy that grew over time.

It's my job to dislodge these *gremlins* by ridding myself of them so that I experience a true healing and not just a temporary solution.

Before The Night, I lived my life in survival mode. Without realizing it. When you've been in any certain state since early childhood, babyhood even, in my case, you simply don't recognize it as anything unusual. It's a way of being. And it affects how a life unfolds—yours, perhaps; mine, definitely. Living in survival mode full-time creates untold mayhem in our whole being.

I'd begun the work of healing my emotional trauma, but in a haphazard way. And without recognizing it as something that called for deep healing. Mostly, I felt I should just be over it, get on with it, stop being a baby about it. Feeling like a fraud for wasting my time and that of others for even remembering events that scarred me, that embedded themselves deep in my psyche, that found homes in my body.

I had impostor syndrome about my pain before impostor syndrome ever became a catchphrase.

In addition, about a year or so before The Event, I came to realize that sometimes, the anxiety, depression, or fear that came upon me suddenly, seemingly for no reason, didn't belong to me. I picked it up from others, like an empath, or through emotional contagion[1], that phenomenon of people transferring emotions, both positive and negative, to others.

Whichever way it came to me, too often, I lived life in a pond filled with the stuff, much like koi fish in a pond full of algae, which can kill them if not controlled.

Life gave me plenty of reasons for feeling anxious, scared, or depressed, but I believe that the *habit* of those emotions—the not letting go of them when their services were no longer needed—was handed down to me by my mother. Unbeknownst to her. And me.

I must now stop carrying the guilt of the adults who harmed me, who continued to harm me well past the time I left them behind because I held on to the trauma suffered at their hands.[2]

It requires going back, back, back, to the negative events that caused the negative feelings that latched onto me, their claws deep in the tissues of my left breast, and that gave birth to multiple myeloma cells running through my bone marrow like crazed

---

1. Kramer, A., Guillory, J., & Hancock, J. (2014). Experimental evidence of massive-scale emotional contagion through social networks. Proceedings of the National Academy of Sciences, 111(24), 8788–8790

2. https://www.anxiety.org/understanding-trauma-childhood-sexual-abuse and https://psychcentral.com/blog/psychology-self/2018/07/abuse-neglect-blame#1

rabbits multiplying fast in the spring, sustaining themselves by eating my bones from the inside out.

The energy associated with the trauma that led to the above must be eliminated. To do so, I must go deep inside myself, go to the source.

Looking back on my childhood, I see my mother as a woman trapped in a life situation she didn't want. She loved my father deeply, this I've always known, but she hadn't wanted children. That's become clear to me as well. One might say it's wrong of me to ascribe this to her, but, after much speculation, I've found no other explanation for her abusive behavior, for her clear resentment at my presence, at that of my siblings', too.

She ended up with five children as a side effect of being married to a Catholic man who didn't understand marriage could exist without children. He wanted the children, but that didn't mean he wanted to help with them. Like most men of his generation, he contributed little to the everyday running of our household. He did no laundry, cooked no meals, cleaned nothing. And this despite the fact my mother worked a full-time job too because he didn't earn enough to raise these five children he wanted. I now believe she felt angry about this, but it wasn't something a woman could complain to a husband about in those times. The world said that household chores went to women, no matter her other obligations. So, she put up with it, and found herself another place to put all that anger: her children, especially my sister and me.

Whether or not you're an empath, you still pick up the emotions of others to a degree. We all do this unconsciously unless we're aware of the contagion phenomenon. When you pick up emotions in this way, you take them on as yours. And gosh did I pick up on my mother's anger and angst! Add that to my own anger at being mistreated, anxiety from always waiting for that next slap, punch, or kick, and my constant fear of her, and what do you get? An angry and anxious girl—and later, woman. All repressed, of course. Which gave the emotions freedom to park themselves in my body and go about doing their thing until they manifested into cancer.[3]

Healing—*true* healing—requires more than the right chemo drug, other pharmaceuticals, supplements, acupuncture, detox modalities, or working with a therapist. Or even a naturopath oncologist in addition to the regular one. All those things in combination do a lot to heal the body, but unless you go back and address the emotions that gave birth to the disease or illness in the first place, it's but a temporary reprieve.

Because matter and energy are separate even when intermingled. Think about two entities sharing the same body in a sci-fi movie. If a surgeon does a lumpectomy or takes your breast because you have breast cancer, *the energy that created the cancer in the first place doesn't leave with the tissue or the breast. It stays.* There are no walls or doors or removal of a

---

3. https://www.purdue.edu/newsroom/research/2012/120717FerraroChildren.html , https://acsjournals.onlinelibrary.wiley.com/doi/full/10.1002/cncr.24372 and https://www.ncbi.nlm.nih.gov/pmc/articles/PMC6036632/

body part that cuts out energy. It doesn't disappear; it just floats about. And that negative energy continues to adversely affect all tissue around it—and grows back into matter again. Just ask the people who've had limbs removed yet still feel them. That's why, unless we make emotional healing a part of healing a disease, just like Arnold Schwarzenegger, it'll be back.

Making use of only tangible ways to heal—a chemo infusion, shot of penicillin, popping a pill or dozens of supplements every day, having acupuncture needles inserted in specific spots to remove meridian blockages, and any other tangible healing modality—is like covering a hole in a bowl with cellophane tape. Before too long, any water added to the bowl starts leaking through the tape. You must repair the hole itself to ensure the bowl never leaks again.

Same with healing. We must repair the emotional damage that brought on the illness, not just handle its current symptoms, not just use cellophane tape on it.

In my case, for my whole life, anxiety, anger, shame, guilt, and fear lived on my left side, principally in my breast *in the exact location breast cancer manifested itself in me.*

Not once, but twice.

It also lived behind my breast all the way to my back and down to my hip area, on the left of my spine, exactly *where my vertebrae broke.*

After my first go with breast cancer, I'd read in a magazine that many people used transcendental meditation as a healing tool, and I decided to try it.

I hired a teacher who taught me a mantra, and I meditated every day, twenty minutes in the morning and twenty minutes in the evening. But I lied to myself, you see. I sat in my chair, closed my eyes, said my mantra, and gently returned to it over and over when thoughts intruded.

It didn't help that the whole time I found myself quashing down the sneaky voice murmuring in my mind that it's not real. It doesn't work. It's stupid. Raised by Catholic parents who practiced superficial prayer, and only in front of priests and nuns, parents who considered religiosity to be spirituality, and who judged anyone who believed any other way at all, I would have to do more than sit on a chair for twenty minutes a day repeating a mantra to get to the fundamental level of what ailed me.

Yet, during the six months I stuck with it, I caught a few glimpses of the unknown where I now know all possibilities exist, the one found in the blackness when we close our eyes and move beyond our ever-chattering mind, reaching out with our feelings.

There lives peace. There lives love. There live all possibilities. Including healing.

But back then, despite those glimpses, I resisted it, perhaps due to residue of Catholic dogma still floating around in the back of my mind even though I'd lapsed twenty years prior. Add to that the children who needed me, the rent calling to be paid, putting food on the table, and I drifted away from meditation. But more than obligations, I now realize that those glimpses scared me. I felt as if I'd entered a room with secrets, secrets forbidden to me, secrets that weren't for me but only for others.

Fast-forward twenty-six years and *whammo*! A diagnosis of not only breast cancer again, but multiple myeloma as well.

Though I now understand *and believe* that intangible modalities such as meditation and various forms of energy healing help turn things around when it comes to illness, I still didn't *feel* it when I first began my meditation journey after The Event.

My mind bought it, but my emotional body ran off into the wilds of nonbelief, of negativity, running as far away from this most elemental way to heal, to thrive, as possible.

It would take me praying for death, and then deciding to thrive instead to force me, finally, to approach everything I did for healing in a mindful manner. To engage with the processes and most important of all, *to find my way to believing that healing is for me, too*, not just others. This shift made all the difference for me.

For most of my life—most likely all of it considering my family of origin—I carried these destructive emotions without thought, accepting them as things that cannot be changed.

Time for a way-delinquent spring cleaning of my emotional body.

To avoid any physical repair work on the body failing in time, among other things, I must deliberately and consistently clean out these negative emotions until no remnant remains. Like invading the core of an apple with a corer to remove it and its cyanide-laden seeds, I must invade my own core and remove these bad seeds from my being.

Because epigenetics shows that cells take their instructions from the energy field around them, not from within, as was once thought.[4]

According to some, this means that it's possible to change the health of a cell just by changing the environment around it. And the one way we can do that is by controlling our feelings, which, after all, are energies that live in our bodies.[5]

We can apparently do this by persistently realigning our thoughts with what we want rather than what we don't want. In time, the new thoughts create new neural pathways in our brains and dissolve the old ones. This, in turn, changes our feelings, which changes the energy around our cells.

As a nonscientist, all I personally can say to support all this is how everything about me changed when I began to meditate with the intent to make myself whole, to align my energy centers (chakras), and to constantly lasso negative thoughts and replace them with their positive counterparts.

As I've said earlier, Dr. Joe Dispenza has his critics, just like anyone with new ideas and theories that start to get traction. But how can we discount the thousands upon thousands of

---

4. https://www.encyclopedie-environnement.org/en/health/epigenetics-how-the-environment-influences-our-genes/ and https://www.ncbi.nlm.nih.gov/pmc/articles/PMC2998160/

5. https://www.ncbi.nlm.nih.gov/pmc/articles/PMC2998160/

people who claim to have been healed by integrating meditation into their healing practices? I'm one of them. I'm not saying that this is the only thing that healed me. I'm claiming that my new mindset, brought on by two years and counting of meditations, is the linchpin that made everything else work. It's neuroplasticity at work. That's all.

Dr. Joe isn't the first one to present these ideas. The "father" of neuroplasticity, neuropsychologist Donald Hebb, is credited with having coined the phrase "neurons that fire together wire together." In 1949.

See how long it takes for woo-woo stuff to get even just a toe into the mainstream doorway?

The process of neurons firing and wiring together means our brains aren't stagnant. Neurons form and wire together, and unwire, depending on our thoughts and on whether we take repeated action on them.

For instance, when you first learned how to drive, swim, cook, sing, dance, to be best at beer pong, etc., the reason that, in time, you did it almost unconsciously is because neurons in your brain—the ones responsible for the physical actions required to perform those tasks—have formed and wired together due to your repeated actions. If you stop performing those actions, in time, those neurons will unwire, and you'll have to refresh those skills.

As a child and young teenager, I ice-skated several times a week while growing up in Canada, and prided myself on being quite good at it. Fast-forward to a day on which I took my children to the first-ever ice-skating rink in Las Vegas, Nevada, where we lived. I hadn't put on a pair of skates in at least twenty years, and for the first half hour, I had to hold on to the railing to make my way around the rink. By the end of our two-hour allotted time on the ice, I easily made my way around it, even doing a couple of twirls.

Bottom line is that pathways in the brain are formed and reinforced through repetition. That's how a habit is formed.

Today, cognitive reappraisal is the term used to describe the act of looking at events differently so that positive, rather than negative, thoughts become associated with any certain situation.

Cognitive reappraisal, for me, means that I think over and over that I am healed and believe that I deserve to heal, rather than being depressed and anxious about this incurable cancer. To my thoughts, I add feeling, meaning I feel the feelings of being one hundred percent healed.

After thinking over and over that I am healed, some of my neurons have wired together on that thought. Each time they connect, it's natural for my feelings to follow suit and suddenly I feel healed. These good feelings affect the energy around my cells. In other words, I'm positively affecting the environment from which they take their instructions. Their environment is now telling them that they are healthy cells. And so, they behave like healthy cells.

Some are highly skeptical of this concept, but thousands have made major recoveries. I know that for myself, none of the other stuff worked well or for very long until I began to engage in daily guided meditations built around this concept. Does it work for everyone? I imagine not. But that doesn't mean I won't continue since it's working for me.

In addition to meditation, I add other energy medicine protocols. EFT (Emotional Freedom Technique), once considered too woo-woo for words, has made its way into the mainstream.[6] EFT can be practiced without the help of a practitioner, though doing a few sessions with a professional helps with getting started.

Also, my therapist uses EMDR (Eye Movement Desensitization and Reprocessing) with me. It helps the brain process and release traumatic memories through eye movements. One can move through what would normally be a dozen sessions in just one. Considering the mountain of traumatic events necessary for me to process, I appreciate that this is like taking the express lanes on the freeway. A practitioner is necessary to make use of it.[7]

These modalities, though now mainstream, are still considered controversial by some, and articles slamming them can still be found online. But remember that the washing of hands before seeing patients and operating on them was also slammed, that Pasteur was ridiculed and persecuted for claiming that

---

6. https://www.ncbi.nlm.nih.gov/pmc/articles/PMC6381429 and, https://eft international.org/

7. https://www.emdria.org/about-emdr-therapy/

germs cause disease, and that incubators were once scoffed at. And we now take all of these for granted.

All in all, it has taken me two years and counting to blast those nasty, unwelcome entities out of my system to a point where they rarely make an appearance.

Out they went, swept away into the quantum soup for the Universe to deal with as it knows best.

This is for Me Too

When I was a young girl, my family would sometimes take outings in our car on Sunday afternoons. My mother liked to visit neighborhoods better than ours and look at the big, beautiful houses there. And always, she would say, "We will never have that, it's not for us, it's just for others." She said this often and with much feeling about many things, not just those houses. Like a mantra. And guess what happens with mantras? Just like any other thoughts, they build up neurons in the brain, sink into the subconscious, which then does its thing to keep the life of the mantra speaker within the boundary of said mantra.

And guess what happens to young children who hear their adults in charge make such pronouncements frequently from an early age? Same thing.

This lesson sank so deep inside me that it became a part of my makeup, went deep into the fabric of my soul, became something that just was.

Once on the road to clearing out my king-sized storage room of negative emotions, I was struck by another realization. To flourish, I must feel worthy of it.

Worthy of death passing me by. At least, until a much later time.

Worthy of living life authentically, of being my true self without shame, without worrying what others think of me, my decisions, my actions. Worthy of a higher purpose.

Before feeling worthy, I must believe in myself, believe I deserve to heal as much as anyone.

I've labored, toiled even, more than most at times, but now in harvest season, I see next to no fruit to pluck off anything anywhere. How can that be?

It can be when one feels undeserving of good things, of great success, because she's heard her mother say so often that it's not for her. It can be when she's been told multiple times in childhood that she's ugly and not so smart, that who does she think she is to even think about becoming a writer, a teacher, a flight attendant, a pilot? Based on that, her unconscious makes sure to sabotage any success above the level of the comfort zone her upbringing placed her in. Even years later, it doesn't even first bother checking with her conscious mind to see if she still believes that she doesn't deserve.

I understand that just because a doctor says something it doesn't mean it will be. I have known this for some time—on an intellectual level—but knowing it emotionally when faced with a devastating diagnosis? Not so easy.

Especially if, like me, you think that great things are not for you, but for others only.

I've *hummingbirded* my way through life, flitting from one thing to another, mainly following my curiosity in my career, flitting from one love relationship to another—only once coming close to true love only to never again love deeply (at least, not yet), other than my children. I partied hard in the early days to kill the pain, the searing pain, traveled to beautiful and sometimes highly foreign places looking for...what?

What, exactly, have I been looking for?

It's taken me all this time to realize that I haven't been looking for anything.

I've been *running* from wherever I've been.

I formed the habit at a very young age (if you've read *Crooked Straight*, my first memoir, you know I ran away from home the first time at age nine) and continued to run my whole life.

I'm a runner.

And, get this. *I've even run away from things that made me happy.*

How's that for screwed up?

I was told so many times in early life that good things weren't for me that now a part of my psyche found it unacceptable for anything beyond *just nice* to stick with me. And though many good things have come my way, I never hung on to them for long because *I knew* that in time they'd leave me, disappear, evaporate, be taken. So, if instead *I* eliminate them from my life (following the urging of my unconscious, who's just doing its job), it gives me a modicum of control.

All those alternative treatments, all those supplements, the herbal remedies, the change in mindset brought on by a form of meditation that thousands of people used to heal themselves, sometimes after doctors sent them home to die. If for them, why not for me?

Because.

At my very core, I didn't believe it would work for *me*. Because my subconscious (again, doing its job of keeping me in the old status quo) *knew* I wasn't worthy of healing at one hundred percent.

Nothing one does to heal, be it chemo, herbs, curcumin, or cannabinoids, or (insert alternative of choice), will work if the user doesn't believe they deserve to heal. Nothing. Chemo treatments will fail, any medication, or alternative treatment, will, in the end, fail. Our powerful psyche delivers to us exactly what we believe we deserve.[1]

The nugget of knowledge that I don't deserve stayed firmly ensconced in the deepest part of me in a hard-to-find place, one I

---

1. https://med.stanford.edu/news/all-news/2017/03/health-care-providers-should-harness-power-of-mindsets.html

barely acknowledged existed. Because accepting it would be too painful to bear.

So, in the end, until my epiphany on The Night, I'd been going through all those various treatments and taking all those remedies only to tell myself I did all I could.

When it only works if you work it from a place of faith and belief.

Nothing happens unless you *become*—before the event occurs—what you want to be, in my case, one hundred percent healthy. Able to move like a person who's never broken her back; like a person not restricted in where and how she lives her life by the need for chemo infusions. Like a person to whom multiple myeloma and breast cancer aren't happening.

But, how can I *become* without the belief of worthiness?

Then, during a meditation, while I'm deep in the field, a voice says to me: "You have always been loved. This is for you, too."

Though I remain in meditation until the end, when I come back to the world, I feel humbled by the pronouncement, and my face feels sticky from tears of gratitude.

Undefinable emotion overcomes me. I feel transformed by the experience.

From that moment on, I've believed it. Healing is for me, too. I accept the gift...

From Invisible to Visible

I'm listening to Chapter Twenty, *Surrender*, of Will Smith's memoir, *Will*, while walking around my house right after eating lunch, setting a timer for fifteen minutes, apparently the ideal amount of time to help control blood sugar, says my naturopath oncologist. I'm glad it has that effect on my body, but I also see it as a great opportunity to do two things I love at the same time in the midst of a busy day: listening to an audiobook and walking. Productive Multitasking, I call it, because multitasking has been proven to be unproductive unless one engages in it through different channels in the brain.[1]

Now, I stop short as if I'd hit a wall. Press Pause on the audiobook. Fumble to pause the timer too. I then place my cell phone on a shelf in my hallway. I stare at it as I would at someone

---

1. https://neuroscienceschool.com/2017/03/06/multi-tasking-costs/

who'd just said something startling. I give the phone my best I-can't-believe-this, surely-I'm-imagining-things look.

You see, I took the lunch and walk break while in the middle of working on this chapter, which talks about changing my personality as one of the things I've done to heal myself emotionally so that I would heal physically.

Anyway, I stop and put the phone down because to my utter surprise, Will has just said that at one point, he hit a crisis in his life where he began to question how he saw the world; about how he lived his life. He said he had to work hard to *change his personality* to fix all the things that made people around him unhappy, but himself most of all.

And I think to myself, *Dude*, I *changed—am still changing—*my *personality! And I've been writing about it in* my *memoir just now. What the f...*

Until I heard him talk about that, I'd never heard of others doing it; I didn't know anyone who had, and I happened upon that chapter in his book at the very time I was writing my own tale of how I changed my persona.

Synchronicity. Confirmation that it's doable because others have done it too. It's energizing.

At some point along my healing journey, I determined to change aspects of my character that do not reflect the self I know myself to be. And I know that there's no way to thrive until I unmask it; because how can I thrive by continuing to be someone that, at heart, I am not? Someone that events in my life turned me into by virtue of feeling the same negative emotions over and over?

My personality is changing due to my work on my emotions via my thoughts. And because now, I believe that healing is for me, too.

But there is more to personality than emotions, and one personality trait that had to go is one I taught myself as a young child. Back then, I developed a persona that revolved around being invisible. It kept me safe. It allowed me to avoid the dangers that lurked all around me in the physical, emotional, and sexually abusive home in which I grew up. I shunned opportunities for fun within my family lest someone (read, my mother) notice and remember to prey on me.

We all become who we must be to heed the inescapable call of survival. But where's the rule that says we can't discard the personality that once saved us but no longer serves us? When circumstances call for a different kind of us?

Continuing to be who we needed to be *Then* often does nothing to help us *Now*.

I wanted to be invisible to avoid being seen by the adults who harmed me on a regular basis. Then, I aimed to escape slaps, punches, kicks, and insults rendered by my mother and parked in my soul to this day. And it helped me avoid some forced visits to my grandfather's bedroom.

My unconscious aim was to float through life on a cloud of anonymity. To remain unnoticed as I walked through my parents' house to avoid my mother taking out her latest disappointment on me with a nothing-that-has-to-do-with-me slap, or down the hallways at school to avoid the unexplainable wrath of Mother Superior, and anywhere else I went so people wouldn't notice my ratty clothes.

Over time, it became a habit, and I subconsciously kept it up through all the hallways of life, tightening my energy as near to my body as possible, taking shallow breaths, my head and eyes firmly fixed on the ground directly in front of me, my mind screaming, *Don't look at me!*

Yet, when in a small group of people I trust, I've always had a natural propensity to laugh out loud, to share stories, to fall in love with people's personalities, be they women, men, or children. Or dogs. I want to be this way with everyone in all circumstances. When in this mindset, my soul feels lifted—and who says it can't be this way all the time?

I love seeing how others perceive the world. Are they interested in quantum meditation? What do they think about the drones on Mars, and would they ever move there given the chance? Is that whole monogamy thing worth it? Have they ever seen the sky at night, far from ambient lights? The kind of sky where the stars are packed so tightly, it looks like a child's dark blue blanket covered with small luminescent dots so close together that when they light up in the dark, they appear to touch one another?

I love telling stories that make them look at me like wide-eyed children, such as about the time I for-real witnessed spaceships in the sky while spending the night at a ranger station in the middle of the crater on Mount Haleakalā on the Island of Maui—and that I'm pretty sure aliens landed that night based on some facts that this story isn't about. I tell them about the time I smuggled thousands of hits of hallucinogenics into Spain back in the '70s—I know, bad girl, but it *was* the '70s.

Oh, and about the time I helped Toronto police find and arrest a vicious serial rapist, but this also doesn't belong here. I mean, I could go on till the end of this book with my stories. But that's not why we're here. We're here to find out how Will Smith and I changed our personalities to change our lives. Well, at least to find out how I did it. He does a great job telling his own fascinating tale; he doesn't need my help.

Personality traits are difficult to change. I believe we only change when the pain of continuing to be the person we know is not the real us causes us more pain than that of changing.

Though it served me Then, in the Now, invisibility serves me not at all as an adult who, for instance, wants to be *seen* by the retinue of healthcare providers who contribute to my continued well-being. If they don't *see* me, if I don't make myself as visible as possible, I'm nothing more than Patient P1234 and the lab results associated with her. Treatment given will be the one offered to the average patient, according to the charts and tables used for that purpose. They won't even ask me if I'm okay with it; they'll just proceed as though I am.

But, like every other human on the planet, I'm unique. Because the charts say that 120 mg of a medication gives good results for the average patient, it doesn't mean it will work best for *me*. For one, as I've already said, my body is hypersensitive to any kind of drug. I *knew*, and said, I don't need the same chemo dosage as the next person for it to be effective. But, until after the night I wished for death, did anyone listen?

Whatever treatments I choose to pursue in order to thrive must be tailored to my own tolerance, to how my body accepts or rejects it.

To be heard, I feel forced to become visible, to expand my presence, my energy field, to speak firmly about my wishes, making it clear without saying that I will no longer tolerate being treated like the average person depicted on a medical chart. A patient who questions everything, who suggests how they want their treatment to go, and who wants to be involved in decisions regarding dosage and frequency of treatment, stands out like Vegas Strip lights on a moonless night to medical providers accustomed to *sheeple*.

Invisibility helps me not at all as a writer who wants to share her work with the world. To thrive here, in addition to addressing my emotional state, I must flip my personality from invisible to visible. On as imposing a scale as possible to accomplish my goals.

Done With being a Good Girl

Despite some of my unorthodox ways when it comes to managing my health, and my somewhat bohemian lifestyle, I try to follow the rules society hands out. Most of the time. Many of those rules are, to me, common sense, and others fall under morality, such as don't kill, don't steal, don't abuse the authority bestowed upon you by a body of power (you know, the one politicians break every day), don't make up stuff about other people (fake news, anyone?), be happy when a friend or family member experiences a windfall or a great event in their lives, like getting a promotion, going on a three-month trip around the world, and more.

Mostly, objectively, I can say I've been a good girl. Mainly, it's because no matter how small my transgressions have been, the emotional backlash from even just sneaking an extra slice of ham into my sandwich came so fast and hard for me that I felt floored at the bottom of a canyon, like Wile E. Coyote after chasing Road Runner. Imagine the emotional backlash from all the dangerous, crazy, and illegal stuff I did in my late teens and early twenties.

With my new resolve to thrive, though, I wonder. Is being a good girl 24/7 such a good idea? Is it healthy? Does everything I resolve to do to heal have to be done every single day, ad nauseum? Because that puts pressure on me, and another word for pressure is *stress*, and stress doesn't belong in my Heal Maryse wheelhouse. And so, I learn.

On dexamethasone and can't sleep? Instead of cleaning the kitchen—a sensible use of this time windfall—why not grab that pint of Cherry Garcia and eat it in bed while reading a good novel, something I haven't done since my early twenties? The ice cream in bed part, I mean.

What's the worst that could possibly happen? My heart will singsong for an hour or so, that's what. Yes, it also means I've done a bad thing by eating sugar, but it's a one-time thing. Even mainstream science now agrees that feeling emotionally happy improves our immune system and our general well-being.[1]

Feeling slumped in the middle of a workday in the middle of the workweek? Leave. I get in the car and drive to my favorite local preserve and walk for thirty minutes or walk the trail in the park behind my house. Cell phone plays music or an audiobook. No emails, no phone calls, no responsibilities to attend to.

---

1. https://pubmed.ncbi.nlm.nih.gov/17027886/

Doing this gives me so much energy, I accomplish more when I get back to my desk than if I'd slogged through the day. For real. As an aside, neuroscience has shown that after about six hours of work, our mind meanders onto easier tasks and looks for short cuts, which could mean doing sub-par work, so a break is productive.

All those wildflowers—red, purple, yellow, blue, thrown together wildly with no care over whether their colors coordinate (yet somehow, they do)—on a summer walk in Breckenridge, Colorado, brought to mind the song "Born to be Wild," the anthem of my youth. I'd heard it again yesterday and wondered whether it had served me well—whether it should have been my anthem at all. Was I innately wild? Or had circumstances driven me to do wild things, like running away from home constantly to escape physical and emotional abuse, something the world, unless they looked under the hood, considered wild behavior?

Despite that some people might think of me as a wild child, even now, I always try to be a good girl. Meaning, I too often do what others expect of me, whether or not it's good for me.

With my new resolve to do things my way, to mindfully handle my healing journey, it means not worrying too much about toeing the line like a good girl, so as to not offend anyone, so no one will think me a bad girl.

Surely doing what's good for me instead of others is being a good girl, too?

Surely it helps with my well-being?

Surely.

Time on My Mind

Did I just shut down a movie I rented online for $5.49, just twenty minutes into it? Yes, I did. I found it boring as heck and I henceforth refuse to waste time on not-entertaining-to-me entertainment. If it doesn't thrill me, I leave.

I could be writing instead, or reading that thriller I started last night, which *does* thrill me.

I feel we too often do things out of duty or a sense of obligation, even when not necessary. Of course, we have to feed the kids, and the dogs and cats, whether or not we feel like it; we have to work to pay the bills; water the plants so they don't die; and keep the front yard looking decent so the neighbors don't think the Addams Family lives here.

But things like watching to the end of a movie because we spent money renting it? Is my time not worth more than the $ 5.49 Amazon won't give me back even though the movie sucks?

You're right. It is.

In the past three years, I've left theaters before the end of the movie; left restaurants after sitting down if the place didn't look that clean or after the appetizer if my taste buds said no; went back to my house on our family property to read a good book when the dinner party got boring for me (my son was hosting in his own house); hung up the phone after too many minutes on hold when trying to order something by phone; and...well, you get the picture.

I saved myself from a few hours of blah time just by doing those things.

Yes, I know, life isn't only about fun, but when death has shared your bed for a few hours before changing its mind and leaving, you realize the preciousness of every minute. And I'm not wasting any of the ones life bestows upon me. Not one.

Death

Into my early thirties, I feared sleeping without at least some ambient light, like the one coming in from under my bedroom door. What did I think waited for me in the darkness? No idea. It's just that panic grabbed me at the thought of closing my eyes and sleeping without light.

My demons waited there, you see, having been held at bay in the busyness of the day. They came out at night to parade around in my head and in the region of my chest, where I felt them most in my body. I thought death would take me while there in the dark at the mercy of anxiety, anger, guilt, shame, all of it plaguing me like a flu that never ends. And dang, did I fear it.

Until the night it almost took me.

Now, I simply live with it as peacefully as possible, side by side, like I live with my neighbors, rules and regulations of society, the absurdities of social media, electric and magnetic fields emitted by my devices (which is essentially radiation), but who's ready to toss their cell phones? Not me. These things I accept because there's no getting away from them. I accept them, while simply doing things to counteract them.

Does death not deserve at least the same? Acceptance? And do we not deserve to do what we can to counteract it?

It's going to happen, no matter how good we are, generous, giving, accomplished, and even no matter how much we work at being the healthiest we can possibly be. The cliché is that no one gets to avoid death. It's clichéd because it's a fact repeated ad nauseam.

And it's repeated ad nauseam because it's true.

So, why are we so intent on trying to escape it? It gets us in the end despite our best avoidance tactics.

In *Death and Dying*, authored by two doctors, Shawn Abreu and Nicole Piemonte, Dr. Shawn talks about a patient whom he helped care for during his residency but who died anyway. The patient, a woman, had, just six days before, chosen to no longer do dialysis with full knowledge that patients who forgo it die in less than eight days.

Yet, when her daughter called emergency services because her mother had become unresponsive (she was going into liver failure), the patient was put through untold pain and discomfort by doctors and nurses trying to revive her. Clearly, she'd wanted to die, was ready to leave this life behind.

Dr. Abreu, shocked by all they had done to the patient to try to resuscitate her despite the whole team knowing she'd die within hours anyway, that her survival chances were near nil, dug deeper.

Later that day, he scoured her medical records for some sort of clue as to why she'd chosen to go without dialysis, the one thing keeping her alive. Finally, he found a note in the patient's chart stating that she'd told her doctor she did not want to die in a hospital, did not want endless treatments because she'd seen the medical pain and turmoil her husband had been put through at the end of his life.

The woman had belonged in a hospice, not in a hospital. There, this patient's last few hours of life would have been more comfortable and spiritual, her transition guided by trained staff.

Perturbed by the dichotomy between her wishes and what was done to her, Dr. Abreu contemplated why the medical establishment puts patients through such pain and discomfort at the end of their lives, even when they clearly don't want it.

He concluded that doctors feel compelled to try to save a life even when the odds of success are nearly absent because it's all they're taught in medical school, all they know how to do.[1]

After reading this horror story, I double-checked my Directive to Physicians, which explains my wishes should I ever end up in a position like that patient. Did that patient have one in place? It doesn't say, but I do know that each time I've been admitted to a hospital, I've been asked if I have one, *but no one*

---

1. https://thereader.mitpress.mit.edu/reckoning-with-medicines-rescue-fantasy/

has ever asked to see it. How did they know whether or not I had one on file with them? How can they honor it on the spur of the moment if someone must go to my house and get it out of my safe? I plan to bring it with me should I ever again be admitted to a hospital, and plan to give a copy to each and every medical office I have to deal with now and in the future.

No resuscitation for me. I'm to go in peace with no regrets over things I might have done, or not done, surrounded by majestic trees and the sound of birds, perhaps a stream or waterfall nearby, and my loved ones around me celebrating the good moments of my life.

Who would choose to die to the sound of beeping medical equipment, and with a tube shoved down their throat to force breathing, doctors possibly cracking or breaking their ribs while trying to get a heart going even if the patient will only be around an extra day or two?

One day, society will see this practice as barbaric, the same way we now look at ancient practices such as bloodletting, mercury and dung ointments, trepanation, and the list goes on.

My children and close friends know how I wish to die. We talk about it frequently enough that I doubt my daughter will ever pick up the phone and plead with emergency personnel to save my life at any cost, including what would essentially equate to medical torture for me.

Since we can't avoid death, perhaps it's high time we acknowledge it, normalize it.

Accept it, talk it out instead of avoiding conversations about it. Make peace with death; get to know her, acknowledge her should you find yourself in the same room with her as I did on The Night. I say "her" because I sense it as a feminine presence, but you can refer to it by whatever gender you perceive it to be.

Now that I've made my peace with death, no longer fear her, recognize her place in the grander scheme of things, I find myself more courageous about living life. Because worst-case scenario, I'll die, and that no longer bothers me.

Repeat Mode

I have difficulty focusing on difficult material when reading books about science, mathematics, medicine, and quantum mechanics. Yet, the subjects fascinate me.

What happens is that when reading something I find difficult to grasp, my mind starts to make a grocery list, or wonders what color sheets to buy at this coming weekend's sale or thinks about what my daughter might be up to this weekend in Nashville, where she's headed for a friend's birthday. In other words, I disconnect from what I'm reading *while reading it*! My mind wants to escape the difficult-to-absorb material.

Then, it dawns on me why one morning as I peruse *The Biology of Belief* by Bruce Lipton, reading snippets here and there (just the kind of read my mind wants to run from). One of those snippets says that *our subconscious mind remembers the action we took during a first-time traumatic or stressful moment and automatically repeats it whenever we come across a similar situation.*[1]

A truth hits me so hard and so vividly, it sears my brain!

I realize that my mind going off into some other place while I read difficult material is most likely a direct result of that time when I was doing math homework at home in first grade, and my frustrated mother picked me up by the neck and strangled me as she hit my head against the wall repeatedly because I'd asked her for help twice; once hadn't been enough. Petrified, my psyche went somewhere else so I wouldn't have to feel my mother's hands around my neck and see the rage on her face. I imagined that the neighbors heard her yelling, heard me kicking the wall, that the police would come and take me away forever. None of which happened.

No wonder that now, when reading anything I find difficult to comprehend, my psyche is taken back to that day. Faced with the same situation—difficult-to-understand stuff—it *expects* a traumatic event to follow, so it shuts down, or goes off thinking about other things the same way it did over that math homework. To protect me. It doesn't matter that nothing traumatic has happened to me since that first time because I didn't understand something I'm reading. My brain learned to deal with that type of situation from that first event and continued to deal with it in that same way each time a similar situation was

---

1. The Biology of Belief, Bruce Lipton, Chapter 7, page 175

presented to it. And each time it did, it reinforced the neuron connections associated with it in my brain.

My *playing* with the many facets of alternative healing rather than working with mindfulness and intent correlates with not only believing it's only for others, but also with my difficulty in processing the more difficult scientific concepts.

So, now I know, but what can I do with this? How can I overcome it? Because a lot of what I read these days to affect my healing pertains to medicine as well as quantum mechanics, epigenetics, neuroscience. It's a slow read because my mind's looking for a way out, so I must take teensy bites with breaks in between.

I continue to meditate, to learn. And continue to struggle with my mind's attempts at escape.

Again and again.

Every time I reel it back in, new neuron pathways form and in time, with many repeats of this action, it will give up its attempts to play hooky. Knowing it will become natural and second nature for my mind to stay on a difficult read helps me keep on track with it.

That's not all, however.

Into Nothing

My spirit flags a little over the constant reeling in of my wandering mind. Still, despite this, I feel a nugget of a beginning of something in following through, like eating salad before dressing was invented. I eat the salad, but sense something's missing.

By chance, or maybe not, I pick up *The Biology of Belief* again, and randomly come across something fascinating.

I become quite agitated. Tears flow down my face. As I continue reading while blinking away the tears, I learn about self-receptors on the cells of our body. According to Dr. Lipton, they essentially determine what makes us different from the next person. If true, it means one can cure oneself of any disease, not just multiple myeloma. Yes, I know this is way out there, even for me!

My disease *must* be energetically tied to my receptors, if what he says is true. If you remove self-receptors from the surface of your cells, where they reside, you become what we might call a generic person. You lose your personality, and any issues, *including health issues*, related to that personality.[1]

Reading that reminds me of something similar I read about a year before The Event in a book by Joe Dispenza, *Breaking the Habit of Being Yourself*. His basic message is this: change your thoughts, which changes your energy (feelings), which changes your life. Changing your feelings changes the energy environment around your cells. So, by changing this, you can change your health.

It seems, based on the fact we can apparently change the environment around a cell by changing how we feel, that the keyword here is *feelings*.

According to Dr. Joe, changing our thoughts, therefore feelings, therefore the energetic environment around our cells is done through quantum meditation.

I meditated his way daily for six months before The Night. I felt some positive changes, such as in my mood, energy, and a lowered level of anxiety, plus more optimism about my future. All this despite undergoing chemotherapy treatments weekly at the time.

Still, though things are now going very well, I'm aware that multiple myeloma isn't fully eradicated from my body. My mind takes me to a place where I wonder if I'm meditating in a wrong way, of if healing completely is just a fantasy.

---

1. The Biology of Belief, Bruce Lipton, page 207-208

During meditation, my mind sometimes goes to the negative such as thinking of ways to properly punish someone who made me angry when they cut me off in traffic, instead of feeling myself whole, feeling as I will feel once fully healed, which is the goal when I start. This is dangerous. Because the cells that comprise my body and my mind then draw instructions from an angry environment. And that's never good. This makes sense to me.

One must focus on high-vibration feelings like love or gratitude, for instance, after first slowing the brain into alpha brainwaves, the bridge between the conscious and subconscious. It's where to go to change habits and behaviors. Also, it's where my mind has stored its need to protect itself from events it perceives as a threat.

If I think angry thoughts while meditating, it reinforces the negativity my subconscious already holds, and negative events will keep coming to me. The brain is like a computer; it just spits out what you feed it. Feed it angry thoughts, and anger-related events find you.

After The Night, and refreshing my memory on this stuff, I realize that more constant higher vibration feelings are the missing ingredient in the salad of my life; the dressing, in other words.

Epigenetics is involved. I'm no scientist as we've established, and I'm sure most of you reading this book aren't either, so I'll keep the explanation simple. Epigenetics is a field of study that falls under the field of genetics. It essentially studies our cells' trait variations caused by *external or environmental factors and behavior*.[2]

Where it was once thought that cells take their instructions from the DNA sequence itself—and therefore there was no way to fix an unhealthy cell—we now know that, instead, we can control our cells by controlling behavior and cell environment.

Have I bored you yet? No? Let's keep at it, then.

So, if environment is also energy, and energy in and around a human is affected by feelings created by thoughts, then it makes sense that thoughts affect the energy around our cells.

And guess what? We *can* control our thoughts, therefore our feelings...

If you've been following, you might have noticed that because thoughts control feelings and feelings are energy and our cells are controlled by their environment, something we can control with our feelings, it means, we can control the environment from which they take instructions.

Worst-case scenario, nothing happens. Best outcome, it heals us. It's worth the gamble.

To change the energy around our cells requires that we go someplace few of us have been, though more people are discovering this every day and changing their health and their lives in huge ways.

To start, we must go into Nothing. Think meditation on steroids. Think a shopping mall for possibilities. They all exist

---

2. https://www.cdc.gov/genomics/disease/epigenetics.htm

there and it's only a matter of deep diving into the subconscious, and from there, plunging into the energy field all around us, or, into Nothing.

I go into Nothing to find my health. To get it back. Not only get it back but become even healthier than before. To thrive. You can go into Nothing and bring back whatever you want.

For many years, I meditated on and off, or rather, did my best to achieve a meditative state, as I explained before. It grounded me even if I couldn't quite get there, and it gave me something on which to latch when Anxiety reared its ugly head.

But meditation as taught by Joe Dispenza is an entirely new experience.

With each meditation, I explore new frontiers, go deeper into territories in my psyche and beyond that I didn't know existed. I'm learning to surrender more each time, especially when able to let go of my body so I become only awareness (the goal here), a move that, at least for me, requires much practice.

I come back with the most precious of treasures: feeling I have a modicum of control over this thing in my body by aligning my energy centers into coherence. Feeling as if I am one hundred percent healed ahead of it manifesting today makes it happen in the real world tomorrow, or at least much faster than it would otherwise.

There is a long list of people sent home to die by their doctors who then embarked upon this work and defied death as a result and to the amazement of their doctors. All those who teach quantum meditation claim such victories.

YouTube has hundreds of videos of their testimonies. Though initially skeptical, after watching a few dozen, I find it difficult to believe they're all making it up. If they're actors, they all deserve an Academy Award for looking and acting just like you and me when something extraordinary happens to us.

I can say that since I started to go deeper into meditation with belief, with mindfulness, with faith, with intent to come out of it whole and healed, and feeling high vibrations only, I've achieved a level of health seen by few multiple myeloma patients. Fewer than twenty-five percent of patients achieve what is known as stringent multiple myeloma status, which means there is no sign of it in blood draws, and no sign of it in the bone marrow.

As of this writing, I'm nearly there, with no sign of it in my blood test results, and less than two percent in my bone marrow. The next step on the multiple myeloma wellness ladder is Minimal Residual Disease Negative, which essentially means no MM cells can be detected in a sample of a million, something measured with a bone marrow biopsy.[3]

Also, my back rarely freezes or gives out nowadays whereas this used to happen several times per week, long after it shouldn't have.

So, off into Nothing I go, each time returning stronger than when I entered, more whole, more confident of my healing,

---

3. https://www.myelomacrowd.org/myeloma/community/articles/multiple-myeloma-remission

feeling quiet joy, peace, and gratitude for being one hundred percent healthy.

My life looks nothing like it did on the morning of The Event, seconds before I broke my back.

My life is different because I am different. And going "into Nothing" has a lot to do with it.

Woo-woo in Real Time

Nearly a year after the mastectomy of my left breast, I'm in the hospital again for breast reconstruction.

Seven people—six surgeons and one nurse are clustered on the right side of the hospital bed on which I lie. They hold their breaths, as do I, as all our senses extend toward a small rectangular box, a Doppler, from which we all hope to hear a specific sound.

The volume on all other medical equipment at my bedside is muted. The Doppler emits static through which we hope to hear the whoosh of blood running through the artery and the veins that have been transplanted from my thighs to my chest.

One of the surgeons, a resident, Austin from Plastics, as he announces himself to me whenever he enters my room, holds a wand that looks like a long thick pen, its tip covered in a clear goo that serves as a conductor for an electrical signal. The wand is attached by a thick wire to the object that holds a place of most importance for all of us right now: that rectangular box.

Austin from Plastics leans toward my newly reconstructed left breast, and as all the other surgeons and the nurse watch, their bodies leaning ever so slightly toward that box, he begins to move the wand slowly along four specific locations on the breast.

If the blood is flowing as it should, behind the basic static of the Doppler, we'll hear a swoosh sound, not unlike waves coming into, and going out from, a beach, but faster. Its presence means that the blood flows well through the transplanted veins. The main artery signal is strong, but the signal for the veins has been declining, again, since three hours or so after the third surgery. A second surgery was needed because the signal disappeared. Same with the third.

We hear nothing.

By now, I've been in the hospital for about thirty hours, at least half of that time under anesthesia. The procedure chosen for me involved removing tissue, skin, an artery, and veins from the top inner and back of both my thighs and moving these flaps to where my left breast used to be.

It's the most complicated of breast reconstruction surgeries, but also tends to have the most success and lasts a lifetime because it involves all my own body parts, rather than extenders and implants. In my case, the latter is unavailable because irradiated tissue (I had radiation treatments during my first episode of breast cancer) has no elasticity, so an extender can't stretch the skin.

The team of surgeons working on me excels at what they do. The head surgeon, Dr. Haddock, along with Dr. Robert Allen, clinical professor of Plastic Surgery at New York University Medical Center, pioneered this method of reconstructing breasts for women who've had radiation and for whom the expander-implant method isn't available. Between the two of them, they perform the highest number of this type of surgery, worldwide. Better hands for me to be in for this procedure don't exist.

Using the Doppler, a nurse and a surgeon have been measuring the flow of blood through the transplanted veins every hour on the hour since my last surgery about four hours prior. A decent flow could be heard at the beginning but measures fainter and fainter with each hourly check.

Now, though, as we all stretch our ears as far as we all can, praying for the telltale swoosh we should hear if the blood flow is good, it sounds fainter than during the last check at two of the spots, and can't be heard at all at the other two that make up the four checkpoints.

Faces remain passive but from my peripheral vision, I catch some exchanged glances between the team. Their poker faces aren't working as well as I'm sure they think.

"So?" I ask.

Austin from Plastics looks me straight in the eye.

"I don't know yet. I need to speak to the boss."

The "boss" is Dr. Haddock.

"He'll decide if we have to go back in."

All the others are looking at him, or at the floor, not at me.

My heart, despite being subdued by opioids and Valium, lets me know it doesn't like this. I feel a sudden compulsion—a strong one—to disappear into meditation. To never come back to our three-dimensional world.

The surgeons and the nurse leave my room, saying they'll be back as soon as the head surgeon decides whether to open me back up, but I know that if the blood isn't flowing, it's the only option.

The vibe, the intent, is that they're leaving now but will soon return to get me ready for Round 4 in the operating room. And this round might mean that the flaps that have been moved might have to be removed and I'll have to remain breastless for the rest of my life.

My impulse to meditate, to disappear from this situation, can't be denied. As soon as they're out the door, I reach for my phone, my noise-canceling headset, and scroll through the meditation playlists on my phone.

The average meditation in which I engage lasts sixty to ninety minutes. Of course, with the team about to return, there's no time for that. Instead, I choose a short, fifteen-minute guided meditation on gratitude as my base from which to dive into the quantum quickly, an iffy proposition, as it usually takes me at least fifteen to twenty minutes to let go enough to get there.

Unlike during my usual meditation, I go into it without my eye mask and meditation shawl. It takes all my focus to set aside my fears about the upcoming surgery, the fourth in less than thirty hours. I feel no compulsion to ask for anything during my time in the void, like for the surgery to be avoided; just a strong desire to leave this moment, this situation, to disappear into the depths of my mind, my soul, to feel that peace.

About five minutes into it, I think of giving up; it feels as if I can't reach the depth necessary to leave my situation.

And that's when everything around me disappears and the show starts.

Something I've never experienced before—no matter how deep or how long I've stayed in meditation—happens.

The world completely disappears, replaced by pastel-colored geometric shapes that travel from left to right in front of my left eye, overlaying one another, appearing, and disappearing, like clouds racing across the sky.

No more than a second or two later, a two-dimensional rectangular-shaped box, divided by black lines into six squares across and twelve down, and with a sepia background, appears, superimposed on the geometric shapes. In each of the squares, mathematical equations come and go. I know little of physics and geometry, but the digits and equations I see remind me of them. They move fast, some within one box, and others seem to slide into the boxes next to them, and back. They move so fast there's no way to focus on any digit, or equation.

A strong urge to surrender, rather than question this vision, fills me. I let go. Observe it for as long as it lasts. Did it go on for only a few seconds? Or longer? I can't say, but suddenly, I once again hear the music and voice guidance of the meditation and realize that, one, I heard none of that during "the show," and, two, the meditation is ending.

How strange. What was that? What does it mean?

I mentally scan my whole body from top to bottom. Things feel different, but there's no time to contemplate how because the door to my room swings open and in comes the head surgeon, his hotshot team of six other surgeons trailing him.

Behind them follows another team: technicians, anesthesiologists, operating room personnel. Having gone through this three times already, I recognize that their purpose for being here is to get me ready for surgery. It's a good thing the room is large enough to accommodate about twenty people comfortably since we seemed to be having a party of the medical kind in here.

My heart doesn't sink at the presence of the surgeons and the OR team. Rather, I feel like the observer of a daytime television drama.

The head surgeon turns on the Doppler and slathers the probe with goo and proceeds to check the first spot.

As if necessary to the process, all of us, our ears once again stretched toward the Doppler, nod our heads in unison when a distinct swoosh fills the air—Eureka!—proof that blood is once again flowing through the transplanted veins, at least in that vein. Some eyebrows go up, discreetly. Mine, not so discreetly.

The surgeon turns his head back toward his team, sharing a brief look with them. I imagine him wondering why they called him in for a nonexistent signal when in fact we can all hear it loud and clear. He then moves the Doppler to the second location; same result. On to location number three; same thing. Location four? Same.

At each spot, the coveted swoosh is strong, even louder than before it began to fade a couple of hours back.

The surgical team exchanges more looks. There's tension in the air. I sense they wonder how they could have missed the signal before, but I know they worked to find it, really wanted to find it; it hadn't been there. That's a fact.

The OR team realizes there will be no need for their services after all, and after a nod from Dr. Haddock, they take a few steps back, and then leave.

I observe all this with surprise, but also with a modicum of detachment.

"Maryse, it sounds fine now. Not sure what changed, but it's good news. We'll just keep monitoring on the hour for a while and hope it continues. In four hours, if things are still stable, we'll start checking every two hours and then every four hours."

"Okay" is all I can think of to say in my stunned state, the mathematical equations still fresh in my mind.

"The only thing is, we'll have to keep you here at least four more days."

"What?" I was supposed to have gone home tomorrow.

"We don't need another close call. To avoid it, we're going to keep you on a blood thinner infusion and give you two units of blood. After four days, we'll transfer you to an oral blood thinner and if after twenty-four hours on that the flow's still going strong, we'll talk about releasing you. You'll have to be on the oral blood thinner for four weeks."

I just nod, in shock, still thinking of my strange meditation experience. The image of that box with the mathematical equations moving from square to square, or within one square only, will keep visiting me even weeks later, and my psyche will struggle to make sense of it, wondering if that's what got the blood flowing again.

I've been nearly one hundred percent healed of multiple myeloma, something that happens to a teeny percentage of those afflicted, fully healed of breast cancer. What many call quantum meditation played a big role in that, but I never thought it healed me on its own. I believe it made everything else work to heal me because of, among other things, its balancing effect on my emotional system achieved by going into my subconscious via said meditation. Which contributed to a healthy environment for my cells. Which boosted my immune system.[1] Which made me whole.

---

1. https://www.ncbi.nlm.nih.gov/pmc/articles/PMC5442367/

I've heard of people having spontaneous healings during meditation, but a part of me always received such news with a wish to believe sprinkled with a large dose of skepticism.

Yet have *I* just had a spontaneous recovery of sorts?

Is that what happened? How did the blood start flowing through the transplanted veins again when it had stopped? Was it a coincidence that it happened immediately after my experience during meditation? Except… I don't believe in coincidences. Cause and effect only.

Of course, I can't tell these good people about my experience; they'd likely question whether the drugs they're giving me are affecting my mind. Or decide to give me more drugs. No matter what, they most likely think that this is just "one of those things."

I badly want them to understand that the energy that created the world might have had a hand in this turn of events. But, despite my belief in our ability to make something like this happen, I feel insecure in my knowledge; am wondering if it's a coincidence. But that's a hell of a coincidence, this picking back up of blood flow gone AWOL immediately after my strange experience.

I'm too insecure, too shocked by this new development to say anything out loud, especially to people with scientific training so deeply ingrained that it leaves no room for the contemplation of intangible extraordinary happenings.

Miracle Shmiracle

During a recent marathon phone conversation with a longtime friend with whom I catch up by phone once or twice a year, we talk about my journey in overcoming multiple myeloma and breast cancer, and about how, in the process, my life got taken down twisty mystical paths I'd never imagined existed.

How I liked my life now better than the one I'd had before.

At this point, it's all behind me. I'm living as the new me, my new upgraded normal.

"You're a true miracle, Maryse," she says.

I flinch.

"A miracle? Nah, I don't think so."

"Well, *I* think you are," replied Susan.

"Well...I don't know."

Her pronouncement surprises me. Something about it doesn't feel right. But, to continue the conversation, I let it go.

Later, long after we hang up, I stare into space, mulling over Susan's pronouncement about me being a miracle.

Then, I realize why it makes me uncomfortable. The miracle is not in me, but in the advances in science. I read somewhere that science is the new spirituality, and after the large role I played in healing myself, I believe it.

I don't want people thinking of me as a miracle.

I'm no different than anyone else struggling with a devastating diagnosis. Anyone can do what I did. The science is here now; but like all new things, it takes quite some time to make it into the mainstream.

So, know this.

There is no miracle.

I just did the work.

Really.

Granted, it's been the most difficult work I've ever done. Even more grueling than giving birth. More than graduating college when I kept coming up with excuses to drop out. More than recreating my mother's Christmas fruitcake recipe with at least thirty ingredients from memory. More than hiking the Nā Pali Coast Trail (one of the ten most dangerous trails in the world) while five months pregnant with my son. Yeah.

But just because something is hard doesn't mean it can't be done. As Glennon Doyle, author of *Untamed*, says, "We can do hard things."

Of course, none of the knowledge we now have at hand means anything unless one does the work. Gurus who tell you that you just need to buy their product to make a change abound. I've lived long enough to know, though. There are no miracles; only science we haven't uncovered yet.

There is much proof of spontaneous healings and bravo to those who experienced it. Religious people might want to ascribe those to their god of choice; however, science is quickly catching us up on how such miracles occur, how our brains can manifest on the outside what we think and feel on the inside.

I'll accept I'm a miracle for doing the work and following through because most of the population fails at this.

In business, they say that if one is willing to do only ten percent more than the rest of the population, that person will end up way ahead of the pack. A leader. Imagine that.

You only have to work ten percent harder than the pack to stand out.

It's not different, in my opinion, when it comes to achieving any goal.

The miracle label bothers me because it takes the power of healing out of my hands, and it gives it over to some faceless god. Which weakens me. Which absolves me of any responsibility for the outcome. Therefore, what I eat, think, feel, and do don't matter. When in reality, all of those matter; so very much.

Also, if we call this a miracle, others brush it off as something impossible for themselves to achieve. However, doing the work to achieve healing is available to everyone willing to put in the work. And that's how I see this so-called miracle of mine.

My recovery isn't unique, unusual, or any kind of anomaly. *It is simply me doing the work.*

Which means, if I can do it, *you can do it too.*

It's ongoing. Keeping oneself healthy of mind, body, and spirit must be part of the everyday for us, or things can go wonky. Especially for those of us who've gone through trauma.

Yes, some do the work and perish anyway. We still don't know why, but I suspect one day we will. Meanwhile, those of us privileged enough to have made it (so far) owe them the courtesy and respect of humbly doing all we can to stay this side up of the soil under our feet.

My goal is to take myself gently in hand, and to give my body all it needs to thrive. I want to explore more and more this crazy thing we call life. Bring on the off-the-beaten-path experiences, the relationships with eclectic people, the strange-to-me foods, the woo-woo stuff that makes life interesting and that even heals us.

I want the chaos, hardship, and pain life sent my way in my past to stay back there, while I live in the custom-made present I designed for myself. That's all.

Of course, no matter how much planning, meditating, affirming, and focusing I do, no matter how mindful and vigilant about what's happening inside me, as I said, sometimes the Universe just wants to fuck with you.

Should that happen on as grand a scale as occurred in my past, I've decided I'll be okay, even if it means going to that place in Oregon. I'm at peace with that.

A young lady who lived in Australia, Holly Butcher, who died of a rare bone cancer, Ewing's sarcoma, in 2018—the year of my multiple myeloma diagnosis—wrote a letter about what she felt was important in life and posted it to social media just a day or so before her death. I couldn't say it better myself, so it's best you read the letter yourself. See the link at the bottom of this page.[1]

I don't believe our lives have to be lived according to how society says they should be lived. We've been conditioned to that, but it's *overcomeable*. We must forge our own path through the jungle we call life. A human life that, compared to the lengths of time various eras here on Earth have gone on, lasts about a nanosecond.

I, for one, am not giving over my nanosecond. It's mine to do with as I please, and I plan to stretch it as far as it allows.

Why allow rules made by others to direct your one starring role, that of yourself in your own life? It's *your* production; you should get to call the shots, not some faceless entity called Society. So there, on a marshmallow.

Leaving life is part of the deal when we're born into it. We come alone (unless we're part of a multiple birth, but even then, we're in a separate body), and we leave alone no matter how full of people our lives are at the time we exit our bodies. No human

---

1. https://www.boredpanda.com/27-year-old-cancer-dying-letter-holly-butcher/

is holding the hands of our souls as we cross the divide between this life and whatever comes next.

I believe our biggest trials in life bring with them the most valuable gifts. If we accept the gifts, learn from the trials, feel humbled by the extraordinary chance of having been "chosen" to receive said gifts, if we allow ourselves to learn the lessons, what we learn and pass on hold the highest value.

This thing could fell me again (it's incurable, they say), but if it does, I'll be able to make an informed decision as to whether to stay…or go. New treatments appear on a nearly daily basis, so my decision would be based on those.

Meanwhile, why not grab all I can out of my time here? Why not squeeze the bejesus out of it like getting the last drop of juice out of the last orange on earth?

Because, really, who the f*ck says we have tomorrow?

Did You Enjoy My Story? You Can Make a Big Difference.

Reviews are the most powerful tool at my disposal for getting attention for my books. It's not financially feasible for me to take out billboards and place full-page ads in newspapers and magazines.

The dirty little secret is that those reviews are even more powerful than a big publisher's ads and billboards. That, and the committed and loyal band of readers willing to write them.

Honest reviews of my books bring them to the attention of other readers just like you.

So, if you enjoyed the book, please click below and leave a review on this book's page on your favorite bookseller's website.

Good vibes and blessings are headed your way right this minute for doing this good deed for your favorite author. (I *am* your favorite, right?)

Just Click Here and it will take you directly to the Review page for the book.

(https://www.amazon.com/review/create-review/?ie=UTF8&channel=glance-detail&asin=1735172189)

For those of you reading the Print version, there is no way to make this easier for you. You can simply go to the book's page at your bookseller's website and leave a review that way. Thank you.

Join My Mailing List and Get Free Goodies

Head over to my website, **https://MaryseLaflamme.com** and enter your email address in the pop-up that says this "Hey y'all! How about signing up for my monthly newsletter?"

If you do, you'll gain access to *Stitched in Deceit*, the prequel to the Carli Cano Mystery Series.

Or, if you're not into cozy mysteries, but enjoy memoir more, **go here** to unlock EXCLUSIVE "Outtakes" from *Crooked Straight,* my first memoir, and get to go deeper into backstory events just touched upon in **the story**."

I will also surprise you every now and again with a free novella, or the first few chapters of a book about to be published, or published long ago, or just published recently. Right now, it's a mystery even to me what I'll be sending!

So. Just do it, okay?

Acknowledgments

It's customary for writers to thank all who helped with a book project, but in this case, really, the first thank-you must go to a disease, two in fact, because without them, this book wouldn't exist. I wouldn't have learned the lessons they taught me. And my life wouldn't have been so rich (so far) without it.

Multiple myeloma is a (supposedly) rare cancer of the plasma cells in the bone marrow. Doesn't feel that way to me and the others who are afflicted. In 2020, worldwide, 176,404 people were diagnosed. Of those, 117,077 died from it. That's more than sixty-six percent of patients. Sobering, to say the least: https://www.cancer.net/cancer-types/multiple-myeloma/statistics

Fortunately—and lucky for me—new drugs come along on the regular, and who knows? One of those might prove to be the elusive cure all of us patients crave: https://www.myeloma.org/multiple-myeloma-drugs

Plus, all the alternatives and the spiritual tools available help extend lives, make the journey more endurable, and even enrich it, as it did for me.

Then, breast cancer, the thing all women fear on some level. This diagnosis, though, took a back seat for me because of the hell on steroids that having multiple myeloma plunged me into. But, for many women, it's its own nightmare and many still perish from it.

The World Health Organization shows these statistics: "In 2020, there were 2.3 million women diagnosed with breast cancer and 685,000 deaths globally. As of the end of 2020, there were 7.8 million women alive who were diagnosed with breast cancer in the past 5 years, making it the world's most prevalent cancer": https://www.who.int/news-room/fact-sheets/detail/breast-cancer

If you want to know years ahead of time whether some cancer cells are brewing up trouble in your mammary glands, consider thermography. It detects areas of higher inflammation in tissue years before tumors form, according to a lot of the literature on it. This is currently relegated to the woo-woo closet by traditionalists.

Other than the two illnesses that changed my life, I thank my children, Paul-Henri and Alexanne, for their kindness, for dropping out of own their lives to come to me when I needed them the most. I love them beyond measure.

I also thank Marion Roach Smith for her invaluable guidance, and David Aretha for his slash-and-kill-those-darlings editing style, as well as Eliza Dee for finding and killing those dastardly typos that seem to burrow and hide in every manuscript. This book would have been a proverbial hot mess without their extraordinary skills.

To all the friends and extended family members who stood by me, put up with me, and who kept on loving me and who still do: THANK YOU. I love you, too.

About the Author

Maryse Laflamme is your go-to gal for mysteries, romance, and compelling memoirs. A globe-trotter at heart, her journeys infuse her stories with rich flavors.

In an extraordinary twist of fate, Maryse defied expectations by continuing to thrive way past her "dead-by" date from an incurable cancer.

She lives on Planet Earth (like most of her readers, go figure!) near her family, and graciously shares her head space with the vibrant characters from her books. Together, they relish traveling, throwing, or attending dinner parties, yoga, meditation, and diving deep into quirky philosophical conversations, as well as going deep into the quantum (don't ask).

Also by Maryse Laflamme

Crooked Straight
(https://amzn.to/3yFm914)

A nearly unbelievable true story that often reads like a thriller, *Crooked Straight* tells of Maryse's unconventional coming of age through early loss of innocence, rebellion, survival, and international drug trafficking adventures from Toronto to Amsterdam to Spain.

But that's just the backstory.

Today, life hands her much bigger problems when, over a five-hour span, she finds herself having to make hard choices, and having a spiritual experience. She might want to help Toronto police in the arrest of a serial rapist. Only thing standing in the way is the warrant for her own arrest.

The Carli Cano Mystery Series

(https://amzn.to/3yHoLve)

Fast-paced and light-hearted, with nefarious activities galore (oops!), Carli Cano welcomes you to *her* San Miguel de Allende, Mexico. After saying *adiós* to the cutthroat New York fashion scene, trading skyscrapers for cobblestones, she opened a thriving women's designer clothing resale shop—expecting peace.

Unfortunately, crimes have an annoying way of finding her—like she's a magnet for mischief—and she *must* solve them to keep her fashionista tribe and her town safe. Much to the annoyance of her *Sargento de Investigación* (detective sergeant) cousin who keeps trying to stop her own investigations.

Then, of course, there's Manuel ...

Join Carli and her friends in an atmosphere brimming with old-world charm, modern-day happenings, and oh, no, too many murders to mention!

If you've been captivated by the mysteries of MC Beaton's Agatha Raisin series, chuckled along with Donna Andrews' Meg Langslow series, and sipped through the suspense of Laura Childs's Tea Shop Mysteries, prepare to be fashionably late to everything else once you pick up this series!

www.ingramcontent.com/pod-product-compliance
Lightning Source LLC
LaVergne TN
LVHW051543070426
835507LV00021B/2382